ENC

"Harvey Turner is one of the better evangelists I have had the privilege of knowing. He personifies what he writes here. This isn't a book written by a man unwilling to wade into the lost world, but by a man who opens his home, uses his time, and lives intentionally in the hopes that men and women will become sons and daughters of God."

Matt Chandler
Lead Pastor of The Village Church
President of Acts 29 Church Planting Network

"Harvey has written a theologically sound and immensely helpful book on evangelism—not just on what it is, but what it looks like in real life. Today, many Christians either do not have unbelieving friends, or the ones who do have no idea how to talk to them. This book stirs up a passion to introduce people to Jesus and lays out a pathway for it. Pastors, Christians, and skeptics alike should read this book and would enjoy it."

Duane Smets
Preaching & Vision Pastor,
The Resolved Church, San Diego, CA

"The test of a book on evangelism is its impact on the reader. Am I going to share the Good News about Jesus more as a result of reading it? *Friend of Sinners* gets an A. Not simply because Harvey is a dear friend whom I respect deeply, or because of the book's very practical insight and helpful advice when it comes to evangelism, or because of its clarity on what the Gospel is (and what it is not). All this is true. But *Friend of Sinners* is a winner because it stirred my heart to do what the Gospel calls me to do— share it! I am going to be more active and intentional in developing relationships with those who have not placed their trust in Christ. I am going to be a better friend of sinners because Jesus was. As Harvey says, 'We lead people to salvation in Christ through friendship.'"

Jim Cofield
CrossPoint Ministry

"Pastor Harvey Turner is one of the most humble and likable guys I've ever met. He's also one of the most faithful and effective evangelists I've ever met. You can't get near him and not be inspired to give yourself more to the work of evangelism. For these reasons, I am thrilled to see he has put his theology and practice of befriending sinners and pointing them to Jesus into this little book. Read slowly, with the intent of applying what you learn—for your sake, for the sake of your unbelieving friends, and for the glory of the Savior."

Tony Merida
Pastor for Preaching and Vision,
Imago Dei Church, Raleigh, NC

"In our complex lives we can forget the main thing. That main thing is knowing Jesus and making Him known. Harvey Turner challenges us to take ownership of the gospel in such a way that we love those who aren't lovable...just like us. Weaving in his own story, he calls us to view ourselves as ones who have been won by the friend of sinners and are thereby sharing the same with others."

Eric Mason
Lead Pastor, Epiphany Fellowship,
Philadelphia, PA

"Pastor Harvey Turner, in his book *Friend of Sinners*, offers a bold and refreshing guide for understanding and doing evangelism. Harvey articulates a biblically-based, relationally-focused, and gospel-centered approach to sharing the good news of Jesus Christ as Savior. This book on evangelism is unique because it provides a wealth of practical advice for sharing our faith with family, friends, and co-workers. This is an excellent resource for new members and discipleship and leadership training ministries, as well as current church staff leaders. If you are a Christian leader, read this book and encourage others to read it as well."

Rich Plass
Crosspoint Ministry

"*Friend of Sinners* is a compelling read with wisdom on how to share the truth of Jesus Christ with the people God brings into your life. Harvey Turner communicates both a passion and excitement for sharing the gospel with the people around him. This book challenges readers to consider how God can use them as well. Using his testimony as a storyline and the gospel as our great hope, Harvey clearly explains why we share the gospel, what the gospel is, and how to communicate it in real life. He also includes a helpful section with questions you are likely to face as you live on mission. God has used Harvey Turner in powerful ways to serve the city of Reno. He is a leader, a model of missional living, and we are well served to learn from him."

Brian Howard
US West Network Director, Acts 29 Network

"'Who is invited to my table?' This singular question resounded in my mind while reading the winsome, but bold words of Harvey Turner, as he called all Christians to the joyous labor of evangelism. The question arose of course as I considered how many 'outcasts' with whom Jesus shared meals and life. In His incarnation, He was a friend to those who were seemingly irredeemable. Through His people, He longs now for nothing less. I've known Harvey for many years, and there are few who so magnificently hold together the wonder of God's sovereignty, and the necessity of His children inviting others to feast at His table. Harvey will lead you to a new compassion, and a thrilling boldness—if you read with an open heart and a humble desire to see Jesus' Kingdom more fully realized."

Pastor Lèonce B. Crump Jr.
Founder, Renovation Church; Author of *Renovate;*
Activist and friend of sinners

"Christians are immature in our faith because of a lack of evangelism. We fear evangelism so we rationalize why we never share Jesus with a lost world. This dries our faith up because a main lifeline to growing into the likeness of Jesus is void from our following. When Jesus uses you to rescue one of His lost children, you will experience joy and faith like never before. We are dying without mission, the vast majority of us have never mentioned Jesus to our doubting friend. We need a passionate and gracious rebuke. We need training and courage. We need this book. I'm praying that Harvey's conversation, his journey, his church, and his writings will inspire many to evangelize and many more to believe."

Tyler Jones
Lead Pastor, Vintage Church, Raleigh, NC

"My friend, Pastor Harv, has blessed us with a personal, practical, and thoroughly biblical tool. As a natural evangelist you can clearly feel his passion and practice of evangelism jumping off the pages. From Pastor Harvey's deeply moving testimony to a host of heartfelt and riveting stories *Friend of Sinners* is loaded with insights that will impact the souls of many. *Friend of Sinners* is a must read that can and should be utilized for churches and ministry leaders everywhere."

Pastor Doug Logan, Jr.
Lead Pastor and Founder of Epiphany Camden
Acts 29 Board Member;
Author of *On The Block*

FRIEND OF SINNERS

AN APPROACH TO EVANGELISM

FRIEND OF SINNERS

AN APPROACH TO EVANGELISM

HARVEY TURNER

LUCIDBOOKS

Friend of Sinners

Copyright © 2016 by Harvey Turner

Published by Lucid Books in Houston, TX.
www.LucidBooks.net

ISBN 10: 1-63296-076-1
ISBN 13: 978-1-63296-076-4
eISBN 10: 1-63296-077-X
eISBN 13: 978-1-63296-077-1

Special Sales: Most Lucid Books titles are available in special quantity discounts. Custom imprinting or excerpting can also be done to fit special needs. Contact Lucid Books at info@lucidbooks.net.

Scripture quotations are from the ESV® Bible (The Holy Bible, English Standard Version®), copyright © 2001 by Crossway, a publishing ministry of Good News Publishers. Used by permission. All rights reserved.

I want to dedicate this book to my wife Rachael.
You are the best evangelist I know.

CONTENTS

Introduction

I talk to many nonbelievers. One thing I've noticed during these conversations is that I have only a couple of times come across people who are not interested in spiritual things and are not interested in God. Sometimes, people put up a front and act as if they don't care about God, but once I start talking with them, I find out they have some form of belief in God and recognize that there likely is a God. I often find they have prayed to him in their own way.

For most people, their issue is not with God—they're even open to the concept of Jesus. What they're not as open to is what they perceive Christianity to be. Sometimes people view Christianity negatively because of the way culture portrays Christianity, so they assume Christians behave a certain way. Or somewhere along the way they met an arrogant professing Christian who completely turned them off. Still other times, they assume that to be a Christian means to join yourself with a right-wing political agenda. Finally, some people have had bad experiences with the church, and they've been burned.

But I've almost never run across someone who says, "I'm not interested in God; I don't want to talk about him. I don't believe in God." Most people are spiritual on some level, and, in the right situation where they feel comfortable, they want to talk about their beliefs.

Even atheists I've spoken with come across as almost too atheistic. They sometimes act obsessed with everyone else's belief in God. If they don't believe in God, why do they care if someone else has a belief in God? If they really don't believe, wouldn't they be completely indifferent to others' beliefs? It seems that, whether consciously or subconsciously, they are wrestling with the notion of a higher being. It reminds me of the old saying, "There is no God, and I hate him."

What I'm seeing consistently in a heavily secular environment is more openness to God and more openness to spirituality; however, I don't see as much of an openness to the Christian faith and the Christian church. Sometimes I hear people say that their impression of Christianity is, "We're going to try to control their lives and tell them what to do." And the problem is that, if someone is already living their life without Christ in it, they feel like they already know "how to live," and they are not interested in someone else telling them how to live. But they might be interested in hearing about what the Bible says about who God is. Consistently, when I speak with non-Christians about Jesus, they are intrigued.

I think the same was true for me when I was growing up—I was interested in God, and always had been. There was never a point where spirituality was not interesting to me or when God was not interesting to me.

My family was in and out of churches when I was growing up and attended mostly Quaker and Mennonite churches. These churches were modernized versions of those denominations and not nearly as strict as their more conservative counterparts. I did hear about Jesus and God in these churches, but it seemed like the only version of God that they gave me was a God who was extremely interested in behavior management. They wanted to teach us how to live a moral life, or what they claimed was a moral life. The Bible stories that we heard were the typical, "This guy's a hero; we need to look to him and be like him." What was always absent was talk about who God is and what God is like and specifically, who Jesus was and what he did.

This was true also in the youth group that my parents wanted me to go to. I went a few times to youth group and always hated it. They usually played silly games. My whole life was about being cool—I was a jock and was becoming heavily involved in hip-hop culture, and I was a teenager. When I showed up and people wanted me to play goofy games, I was simply not going to participate.

Another reason I hated it was that they taught only moral lessons: 4 principles for this, 3 ways for that, why you should remain abstinent. There were two problems with the "be good" message. First, I had no desire to be good. Everything I desired was not good. I desired to enjoy my life and escape what I didn't like in my life. I mostly pursued girls, sex, and getting high because there was something majestic about it. But when I went to church, there was nothing majestic about it. It just seemed boring and cheesy. Second, I had no ability to be good, and I knew it. I wasn't going to even try. While I loved the idea of God and was always intrigued by Jesus, I assumed Christianity was about religious obedience.

One more thing that bothered me about this church. At the time, I didn't know Jesus and was naturally self-righteous and full of myself. But I do remember wondering why we never talked about God. I even told my parents, "I don't want to go back. They don't talk about God, anyway. They just want to talk about not having sex and not smoking and not drinking." There were plenty of pleas from leaders to stop my sins or to do the right thing, but I was not interested. To tell the truth, I was there only for the girls. After the age of fifteen, I stopped going to church at all.

As I mentioned earlier, I was heavily into hip-hop and rap. I had been into rap all the way back to the time I was 10. From the age of about 16 to the time I was about 21, I was a rapper. I used to rap at parties, clubs, and different events. As my high school years progressed, I dug deeper into the lifestyle of hip-hop—partying, doing drugs, and eventually selling drugs.

I was arrested several times. The police arrested me for fighting, marijuana possession, possession of drug paraphernalia, and contributing to the delinquency of a minor (the cops showed up to a party I was at, and a couple of people there were under 18. I mouthed off to the cops, so they arrested me instead of arresting other people).

There were times I should've been arrested for actually having drugs with intent to sell, and there were a couple of times I had enough drugs on me that would have sent me to prison for a very long time; however, by God's grace, I was never caught any of those times. I was only arrested for smaller offenses, even though I was involved in some major crimes.

Yet, even during those years, I was always interested in God, and specifically in Jesus. I simply didn't know enough about him because all of my youth I had heard only scattered, disconnected stories about Jesus. I knew he had fed 5,000 people with little food and had walked on water, but I didn't really understand the gospel. I'm confident I heard that Jesus had died for people's sins about 100 times, but I didn't understand what that statement meant.

Even during my rebellion, though, God was moving in my life. Around the age of 20, I began to experiment with harder drugs. I had smoked only marijuana up to that point, but I soon started using some harder drugs like cocaine. If I handled marijuana right, I could live a normal life. But these harder drugs started affecting my job and my relationships.

Another wakeup call was that I had a son at the age of 19. I knew I wasn't raising him well, I wasn't as involved with him as I should have been, and I'd begun to realize I needed to take responsibility for him. I knew my life was not heading in a good direction.

The last straw for me was jail. The first couple of times I got arrested, I didn't have to stay overnight in the jail, and it wasn't that scary. If anything, it became a badge of honor on the street. In hip-hop and street culture, there's often pride in having gone to jail. Being arrested gave me a little more street cred, and because I'm a white guy, I needed that credibility among my friends; however, when I was 20 I had to stay overnight in jail for a couple of nights.

I had hit my breaking point. The reality of jail scared me—I knew I didn't want this for my life. As I was spending those nights in jail, I started thinking more about God. After I was released, I decided to see what was in the Bible my parents had given me.

I was intrigued by Jesus' words. He was perfect, yet not self-righteous. He was accepting of people like me. He was holy, but also humble. He talked about the difference between outward law-keeping and inward righteousness. He spoke of mercy for the oppressed and the sinner. And I sensed such a majesty about his person and character. This majesty was what I had been looking for in all those things I pursued before, and I knew it. This pursuit of him felt pure. It made me feel whole.

You see, I was not looking to Christianity to "get my act together" because I knew morals alone would not work for me. I needed something bigger. I needed to be captivated by God. That's why I had been attracted to music, partying, and girls—these pursuits were exciting and there was something big about them. Until that point, nothing I had been told about Christianity seemed exciting or worth my attention.

As I contemplated Jesus Christ, read his words, and watched his actions and his death for sinners like me, I was pulled in. I finally started to see the majesty and love I was looking for. His sacrifice compounded my intrigue of him and sealed the deal—I began to develop deep affections for Jesus. I truly believed he had risen from the dead. And when a man rises from the dead, you kind of have to give up your whole life and follow him. So I did.

Over the course of the next month of working through what the Bible taught, I became a Christian.

I became a Christian because I was exposed to the gospel of Jesus.

A FRIEND OF SINNERS

My behavior, just like with pretty much every new believer, lagged a little behind what I was starting to understand. But what was different, very different, was my hunger for the word and my prayer life. I started praying all of the time. Before, I prayed only when I needed something. But now, prayer was more about simply worshipping God and wanting to know him. It was very different.

I still smoked pot for a while, but as the weeks progressed, I read the Bible avidly, started attending church, and started going to church gatherings almost every night of the week. I was in multiple churches and multiple different Bible studies. Every night I didn't have my son, I went to a church function, and I began listening to sermons on the radio. I read through the New Testament twice and the Old Testament once within the first three months of being a Christian. I was consuming everything I could.

About a month after my conversion, I remember standing on my front porch looking up at the stars, and realizing God was there. He was vast, and he had been with me through every stage of my life. And I realized, "Wow, I'm fully into this." This was now my life.

I started a Bible study so my friends could hear about God and because they wouldn't come to church with me. It began as a small group of seven guys, including myself. There were two and a half Christians and three and a half non-Christians (I'm not sure if one of them knew Jesus yet). I simply taught through passages of the Bible I knew and showed my friends how Jesus is the Savior. More and more non-believing people began to attend and eventually came to believe in Jesus. In those early days, we met at a party house, and there were still beer cans on the balcony, bongs in the garage, and pornography in the bathroom. But eventually the owners of the house met Jesus and the atmosphere changed.

As the Bible study grew, we submitted ourselves to a local church, and eventually our community planted a church out of that church called Living Stones. That little Bible study has now become four churches scattered across northern Nevada. We have the same mission to be a Gospel-centered church existing to make friends of sinners and, in turn, to teach them about Jesus.

But at the time of the Bible study, it wasn't long before I began to wonder why no one had ever told me much about

God and what he did for sinners. I remembered plenty of conversations about my morals, how bad I was, and what I "should" do. But nothing about Jesus. It was all law and no gospel. Before I was converted to Christ, no Christian had taken the time to tell me about God and the actual person of Jesus. I thought the Holy Ghost was some kind of ghost that lived in heaven.

Why, I wondered, were so few Christians telling people about Jesus?

I've given this question much thought over the years. As I've watched churches and Christians, I've seen a contrast between what Christ exemplified in the New Testament and how many believers live their lives. The religious people around Jesus constantly criticized him for hanging around sinners. Even his disciples in John 4, upon seeing Jesus talking with a sinful woman, questioned, "What are you doing?" They still hadn't gotten it yet.

Over the course of his ministry, Jesus kept bringing his disciples around sinful people, people outside of God's covenant and grace. He was teaching his disciples to do that as well. As the apostles went out into all the world following Christ's death and resurrection, they went out to people who didn't know God and brought the gospel to them, befriending them and seeking to understand them. You see, the pattern in the New Testament consists of being a friend of sinners. But as Christendom developed in the world, Christians began to allow the culture of Christendom to form the ethos of the Christian relationship with outsiders rather than letting Jesus and the apostles form their understanding of these things. The subversive ethos of many Christian movements has become, "Well, we're the holy people, and they're the bad people. They need to do the work of coming over here. We don't need to do the work of going over there." This is not the biblical pattern. The biblical pattern is, "We go to them; we don't expect them to come to us."

You see, many believers today misunderstand what holiness is. Jesus is the most holy person who ever lived, yet he constantly spent time with unholy people. Sometimes, it seems, Christians have a subconscious belief that sin is contagious, and if they hang out with a nonbeliever, they'll "catch" their sin. And Christians certainly don't want other people to think they're backslidden if they're seen with unbelievers. Some Christians would cringe if their Christian friends asked, as the disciples and religious people asked Jesus, "What are you doing?" However, holiness is not something that can be affected from the outside in, it's something that comes from the inside out. Jesus had a heart of compassion for people who didn't know God, and it caused him to reach out to them and befriend them. Jesus gave us a pattern of constantly hanging around these people. He gave us an example of being a friend of sinners.

Another reason Christians don't evangelize is that telling people about Jesus feels uncomfortable and inconvenient. It is much easier to be around people who have the same convictions and values you hold. Everyone is busy, and everyone has enough discomfort in their lives, so why add more?

But...

This is what Jesus sent us to do—he sent us to evangelize. As it says in 2 Corinthians 5:8, "Christ reconciled us to himself and gave us the ministry of reconciliation." Once Christ has reconciled us, he then charged us with telling people about him so that they also can be reconciled. But how do we go about this ministry of reconciliation?

I talk to a lot of Christians who understand that they "should" evangelize others, they understand why evangelism is important in the mission of God, and they even desire to obey Jesus and the apostles as they commanded us to spread the gospel (Matt 28:18–20). However, most Christians don't know *how* to do evangelism. That is what I would like to share with you in this little book. Much of this book comes from my experience in being a friend to sinners. I have seen many of these sinners become disciples, deacons, pastors, and church planters. I hope what I have to say here will help to demystify evangelism for you and show you how you can befriend non-Christians and help lead them to the Friend of sinners, Jesus Christ.

WHAT IS EVANGELISM?

Before jumping into the main part of the book, it's important to establish a clear definition of evangelism because people have conflicting ideas about its meaning—the word has become dysfunctional in its modern use. The word *evangel* literally means "gospel." The Greek word *euangelion* means good tidings, or joyful news, and in the story of the Bible, the word refers specifically to the good tidings and joyful news about the kingdom and salvation that Jesus brings to humanity. The gospel is the news about Jesus: his life, death, resurrection, and kingdom.

I have a made up word for evangelism. Evangelism is kind of like saying "gospel-ism." To evangelize is to "gospel" people—to bring the historical realities of the gospel to bear on the lives of individuals. This is what it means to be a Christian: we have been "gospeled" by God's grace because of other Christians "gospeling" us. So, we Christians "gospel" each other, and "gospel" those without this gospel. We bring the news of Jesus to bear on the lives of our friends and family that they might share in the joy of the love of God. That is what I mean when I say evangelism, "gospel-ism."

To explain it another way, evangelism simply means to apply the gospel to people's lives. Since the gospel is about God's free grace, applying it to nonbelievers means taking that concept of free grace and helping people to see how it relates to their lives—the way they think, the way they feel, the way they spend their money, the way they conduct relationships, and the way they do marriage. Evangelism is applying God's gospel to their sinful condition: separation from God, spiritual confusion, and a broken relationship with God. This gospel gives them the pathway to communion with God. When you do apply the gospel to non-Christians, you are evangelizing or "gospeling" them.

Evangelizing people isn't about getting non-Christians to start acting right. It's helping them understand what Christianity really is. Christianity is centered on Jesus and his life, death, and resurrection. The gospel is not about being perfect because you can't be perfect. This truth is what brought me in. When I started reading Jesus' actual words, reading what he actually did, reading his compassion, and reading his character, I wanted to know more. For most of the people I've led to Christ over the years, this is the same truth that draws them in.

IS EVANGELISM FOR ALL CHRISTIANS?

Are you a disciple of Jesus? If you are, then you are called to evangelism. We get to deliver the greatest news in the history of the world—that God has made peace with the world through his Son. I can't tell you how many times I have talked to Christians (even pastors) who have told me that they don't "feel" called to evangelism. Do you allow your feelings to trump the Great Commission? Others talk about not having the "gift" of evangelism (Eph 4:11), and of course, I would agree that this gift or office in the church is only given to some. This book is about you playing your part in the worldwide evangelistic mission of God.

The call to be a disciple of Jesus is a call to evangelism. When Jesus called Simon and Andrew to discipleship his call was "Follow me, and I will make you become fishers of men" (Mark 1:17). If you want to be Jesus' disciple it seems that he wants to make you into a fisher of men. It's pretty simple: fishermen fish. Disciples of Jesus evangelize. Disciples make disciples. This statement of Jesus is found in three of the four gospels right at the beginning of his ministry (Matt 4:19; Mark 1:17; Luke 5:10). It functions as a sort of vision statement of the call to follow Jesus. So whatever your vision of the Christian life is, it must include evangelism as its mission. As the great British preacher Charles Spurgeon observed, "Every Christian is either a missionary or an imposter."[1]

Having said that, I would point out that not all Christians will have the same level of calling, giftedness, opportunity, and desire for evangelism. That is ok, as long as you are willing to be available to God in the way he wants *you* to be part of the evangelistic mission. Some of us may talk to thousands about Christ and see hundreds of conversions, and others will share Christ with three or four neighbors or co-workers over the next few years and one will meet Jesus. As long as you are available to Christ for what he wants of you, you are free to run *your* race and contribute to the ingathering of "the children of God who are scattered abroad" (John 11:52).

This is the bottom line. You live in a particular neighborhood in your city. You work a job among other co-workers. You have neighbors, friends, and family. You live in this particular place and time in history because God has a purpose for you. He saved you because he loves you, and he wants to send you because he loves others. God has children he wants to bring into his family here and now. I am here to fish for men and women that they might be reconciled to their great God. God has determined to save his people, and I am delighted to be part of finding the lost sheep. This is true for you as well. God will send you as his child to find our lost brothers and sisters.

THE LAYOUT OF THIS BOOK

In the first three chapters, we will discuss the foundational components of evangelism. These three chapters serve as the "why" behind the "what." These three chapters are probably the most important. The next five chapters are the "what" behind the "why," or the how-to's of evangelism. The last three chapters are the "how" to implement the "what." Throughout the book, you'll also see **#evangelism** quotes to share on social media.

Before we begin, I would invite you to recognize that if you take the concepts in this book seriously, you are walking on holy ground. It is holy ground because this is what is on God's heart. This is what he sent us to do, to tell the world about Jesus. (Matt 28:18–20; Acts 1:8) If you would, just take a moment and pray with me.

> *Heavenly Father,*
>
> *I love your Son, the Lord Jesus, and by the power of your Holy Spirit, I want to tell people about him. Help me understand what I need to understand as I read this book so that I might reach those whom you've called me to reach. I pray this in the name of the Father, and of the Son, and of the Holy Spirit.*
>
> *Amen.*

CHAPTER 1

Friend of Sinners

Do you like sinners? Jesus did and still does.

LIKE SINNERS, LIKE JESUS

I hear many Christians talking about personal holiness. They talk about being like Jesus, being conformed into the likeness of Jesus, walking like Jesus, and following Jesus. But most Christians I know don't love sinners like Jesus did. They don't hang out with them, they don't share the gospel with them, and they just plain don't like them. But could it be that the process of becoming more holy includes hanging around those who are considered *un*holy?

I believe some people in the church have a flawed perspective of the meaning of holiness. Many understand holiness as separateness from others. Here we are over here doing our church, Sunday school, Bible studies, and all our holy activities. Most of this is necessary, but the whole point of church activity is to make disciples of people who are not. Christians are called to reach out to the un-discipled. And the church exists as a mechanism for God to reach out to the world, not as a holy huddle gathered in a corner. So maybe a common understanding of holiness as cloistering away into a holy club is antithetical to true holiness. Instead, these holy huddles can be evidence of disobedience. When we close ourselves off from the rest of the world, we do the opposite of what Jesus did when he reached out to those deemed "unholy." Almost any chapter in the gospels will prove this.

JESUS WAS A FRIEND OF SINNERS

In the gospel accounts, the religious crowd accused Jesus of being "a friend of sinners" (Matt 11:19). He was known to hang out with people who lived overtly sinful lifestyles. The Pharisees, the religious leaders of the day, said, "This man receives sinners and eats with them" (Luke 15:2). Jesus was seen with sinners, spent time with sinners, and knew sinners to the extent that the Pharisees thought he was a sinner as well. In the words of Matthew, "As Jesus reclined at table in the house, behold many tax collectors and sinners came and were reclining *with Jesus and his disciples*" (9:10, emphasis mine).

In the first century, eating with someone meant welcoming him or her as a friend. Jesus once attended a dinner at a Pharisee's house where he welcomed the love of a notoriously sinful woman. It would have cost him his reputation in the eyes of some people; however, Jesus didn't care that people were against his spending time with sinners—in fact, he made a point to contradict clearly what everyone would say about his reputation. To the surprise of the Pharisees, he proclaimed the sinful woman to be a model of faith and forgiveness (Luke 7:36–50).

Jesus would go on to be accused of being the friend of everyone from tax collectors to prostitutes, categories of people that cover the entire social spectrum of rich and poor.[2] You see, Jesus was an equal opportunity sinner lover. Jesus even loved the worst kind of sinners—the religious kind. He ate with them and pursued them even though they would eventually kill him. Now that's commitment to befriending sinners!

JESUS DIDN'T REQUIRE HIS DISCIPLES TO COMPLETE A MORALITY CHECKLIST

Jesus showed an even deeper example of befriending sinners. The biblical text doesn't say Jesus tolerated sinners only if they got with the Christian program quickly. Jesus didn't require his disciples to start "dressing like a Christian" (whatever that means), and they didn't stop using the list of words that Christians disapprove of—although there is no such list in the Bible. They didn't suddenly begin voting for the right candidate. You see, Jesus didn't require his disciples to polish the exterior of their life in order to appear to be a Christian. The gospels never show Jesus turning people away from his gatherings because they hadn't stopped sinning. Rather, the disciples continually questioned Jesus. They often didn't show compassion toward the people Jesus befriended. Judas Iscariot would betray Jesus and, for thirty pieces of silver, turn him over to be killed. But Jesus didn't stop spending time with the disciples because they were imperfect, at times annoying, and some would eventually turn against him.

Instead, the gospels tell us that he was a friend of sinners. He knew sinners, went to their houses, and talked with them over wine (yes, Jesus drank alcohol with sinful people). He knew their names, their kids' names, their aspirations and dreams, and what interested them. He was interested in people—like a friend would be interested.

FOR THOSE WORRIED ABOUT APPEARING HOLY

All this talk of cleaning up your act and walking the Christian walk is often termed "sanctification," the theological word for "becoming more like Jesus." But why don't we ever talk about sanctification in terms of being a friend to sinners? Are we really growing in sanctification if we are not following in his footsteps by building relationships with the broken (1 Pet 2:21)? Why do we think it's okay to hang out with only Christians and never with anyone who doesn't believe what we do? Our mission from Jesus is to make disciples of people who are not currently disciples (Matt 28:18–20). Isn't a disciple one who follows his teacher? If we are not friends to sinners, we are not following him. This chapter is an invitation to follow Jesus in this area of our lives, too.

I've heard many Christians say, "It is important that we remain holy." It's as if they are afraid to hang out with sinners because they don't want to catch a sinner's disease (as if you could catch sin like a cold!). Jesus was holy, but his holiness caused him to reach out to people whom the culture deemed sinners, criminals, adulterers, fornicators, offenders, outlaws, and materialistic.

SINNERS COME FROM ALL WALKS OF LIFE

Being a friend of sinners doesn't necessarily mean befriending only the outcasts of society and hardened criminals. It could also mean being a friend to a soccer mom who has her priorities all wrong or befriending a guy on your block who worships his favorite sports team or lives for his career. Maybe you befriend someone from a different religion or the atheist at the pub who despises Christianity. Jesus was known to hang out with these types of crowds, so much so that people accused him of being a drunkard and a glutton (Matt 11:19). The Pharisees said of the company he kept, "If this man were a prophet he would have known what kind of woman this is who is touching him, for she is a sinner" (Luke 7:39).

For the most part, the religious crowd hated Jesus; he didn't keep their rules. One of their greatest complaints was that Jesus didn't tend to focus positive attention on them (the Pharisees and Sadducees). He hung out with those who were sick and blind—the same people the religious folks thought were being punished by God. Jesus' ministry was doubted because of his association with sinners, and if you choose to be obedient and hang around sinners, your ministry will be probably be doubted, too. But evangelism pushes you out of your comfort zone. Language, culture, raw honesty, and blatant sin will likely make you uncomfortable. Persist.

TRANSITIONING TO BEING A FRIEND OF SINNERS

Now whose side are you on? If you were to look at your life, look at your church, maybe even look at your movement or denomination, would the legalistic religious crowd accuse you of being a friend of sinners, like Jesus? Why or why not? If not, repentance is in order.

I've needed to repent of this many times in my life. It's much easier to hang out with people who have the same morals and believe the same way you do. But, if we do not attract the same type of people that Jesus attracted, we might not be on the same mission Jesus was on. This is something we need to consider seriously. So much of Christian culture and church life is inward-focused and unlike the rhythms and relationships that we find in the gospels and epistles. The New Testament is unswervingly outward in regard to its mission. Are you?

But how will you be able to make the transition to being a friend of sinners? First, remember that you are as sinful as every sinner you meet. In fact, you might be worse—look at the 10 Commandments. You regularly break all 10 in thought, or word, or deed. Look at passages like Ephesians 2:1–3—"You were dead in trespasses and sins." If you're still not feeling your sinfulness, you might read through the Sermon on the Mount, where Jesus takes God's laws and shows how they expose the darkness in our hearts. Jesus did this so we might see our need for grace. When we see this need for grace, we're more prone to be gracious to people who do not have it. If you dare take a deep look inside, there is enough in your heart to condemn you right now, and you know it. You are not any better than the sinner next door.

THE CROSS LEVELS THE PLAYING FIELD

Now consider the cross of Jesus. Use your imagination to travel back two thousand years. There Jesus is, bleeding for you. All of your sins, guilt, shame, and failures are upon him. It's a bloody sight, but don't turn away. Don't leave yet. Spend time there at the cross. Remember his perfect life as he bleeds. Why is he there? He's on that cross because he is a friend of sinners— sinners like you. As John 15:13 states, "Greater love has no one than this, that someone lay down his life for his friends."

Do you get it? Every sinner (including you and me) needs the friend of sinners. As new friends of Jesus, he sends us as ambassadors of the embassy of heaven. As the Apostle Paul says, "We are ambassadors for Christ, God making his appeal through us" (2 Cor 5:20a). And this is what we say to our friends who are sinners like us, "We implore you on behalf of Christ, be reconciled to God! For our sake [us sinners] he [God] made him [Jesus] to be sin who knew no sin [who was perfect], so that in him we [me the sinner, and you the sinner] might become the righteousness of God!" (2 Cor 5:20b–21).

Once the gospel moves you to see that you are in need like the people you aim to reach, being a friend of sinners is no big deal. Suddenly you are free to love them as they are, not as they should be. Remember that the only thing that makes you different from an unbeliever is God's unmerited grace.

So how exactly did Jesus befriend sinners? Study the gospels and you'll quickly find he had many approaches for many kinds of sinners. Let's take a look at one in particular.

HOW JESUS MADE FRIENDS WITH ONE SINNER (AND HOW WE CAN TOO!)

The first observation is that Jesus' life and ministry was attractive to people outside of the believing community. In Luke 19, Jesus entered a town called Jericho where a notorious sinner named Zacchaeus lived. The Scriptures tell us that Zacchaeus "was a chief tax collector and was rich" (Luke 19:2). Zacchaeus was intrigued by what he had heard about the ministry of Jesus. In fact, Zacchaeus was so intrigued by Jesus, he went to the trouble to climb up a tree in order to get a glimpse of him (the text tells us he was "small in stature"— he was short).

The Christian community doesn't tend to generate this sort of curiosity for unbelievers. Church communities are not usually known for being attractive to notorious sinners—no one's going out of their way to be a part of our communities. In fact, it's assumed throughout our culture that Christians want nothing to do with notorious sinners. We actually spend a lot of time and energy separating ourselves from them and making sure they are separated from us. This is especially curious because it is unlike our Lord. As we've established already, he was most often attractive to the worst of sinners. Sinners were intrigued by his life, his love, and his mercy. When they heard him speak and saw him act, they were drawn to him, not repelled from him. If your life or ministry does not draw the same type of people that Jesus drew, ask yourself, "Am I on the same mission Jesus is on?"

ZACCHAEUS WAS A CROOK, BUT JESUS LOVED HIM ANYWAY

Zacchaeus was despised for working with the Roman government, a government that supported a system of idol worship. Zacchaeus likely did all the other notorious sinful behaviors—drinking heavily, keeping company with prostitutes, and gambling. But Jesus looked up at this man in the tree and said, "Zacchaeus, hurry and come down, for I must stay at your house today" (Luke 19:5). Jesus called him by name, called him to come near, and asked him to come quickly. He not only asked to visit his house, but asked if he could be his overnight guest. Jesus was making a statement that was clear to Zacchaeus, to everyone who was standing nearby, and to everyone who reads this passage. Jesus came to save sinners. Jesus loves sinners. Jesus redeems sinners. If you are a sinner, Jesus is glad to come over to your house. Jesus likes to be seen with sinners. Jesus does not mind offending religious people. To be a disciple of Jesus is to be a friend of sinners in the same way.

One of my friends, who is a great, friendly guy, is considered a local celebrity with much influence, and he is known for his business skills and achievements. But he is also a notorious sinner in my city. Many know him as a womanizer and a cocaine addict. I've gone to lunch with him and had him over to my house on a number of occasions, and I've received some questionable looks and inquiries. Those concerned with the company I sometimes keep seem to miss that they are just as in need of grace as he is. I just want to introduce him to Jesus. I know they are probably questioning my character for hanging out with him, but I'm striving to follow in the way of our Lord Jesus.

JESUS SPENDS TIME WITH THOSE WHO UNDERSTAND THEIR NEED

In another place, Jesus states that he came for the sick (Luke 5:31). He even goes beyond that by saying he didn't come for those who are well. Of course, he means those who *think* they are well. He comes for the most broken and the most sinful. He even comes for those whose sin has made them a social outcast.

I live in Reno, Nevada, a city known for its notorious sin: gambling, legalized prostitution, strip clubs, drugs, and drunkenness. As I've done a bit of travelling, other pastors and Christians have questioned me on the "wisdom of such a move." They're not so sure I should be planting a church and raising my family in such a place. Even in my city, we planted a church in the urban core right in the middle of all the problems, across the street from a strip club. When I read the gospels, I have no doubt that Jesus would be interested in places like Reno. He would befriend the strippers, drug dealers, bartenders, prostitutes, tattoo artists, casino workers, and anyone else that Christian culture might not readily accept without a good bit of cleaning up.

In our passage, notice that Jesus doesn't tell Zacchaeus that he needs to get his act together before they can be friends. Rather, he makes friends with him in the middle of his sin and leads him to the way of salvation. Zacchaeus hurries down from the tree, greets Jesus, and takes him to his house.

Of course, the religious crowd grumbled, "He is gone to be the guest of a man who is a sinner" (Luke 19:7). There is a modern-day equivalent of this among church folk too. If you commit yourself to being a friend of sinners, religious people will grumble. They will even pull Bible verses out of context, and quote the King James Version, an outdated (and now inaccurate) translation that speaks of "avoiding the appearance of evil" (1 Thess 5:22),[3] so that they can try to get you to not do what Jesus did. All of this is done in the name of being a good "Christian."

I've even heard people say, "Well, of course Jesus can hang around sinners—he is God." They go on to say that we should do the opposite of what Jesus did in this scenario because we might "fall into sin" ourselves. There are a couple problems with this.

First, I would question which is more important: your opinion or Jesus' example? My friend, I know you are only looking to live a holy life, but in order to do that, shouldn't you be following Jesus as your Messiah and committing to being his disciple? I want to pattern my life after his holiness, instead of being a person who thinks they can catch sin like one would catch a cold.

The second problem is, the idea of getting infected by another's sin isn't biblical anyway. So let the folks who are too religious for Jesus grumble away. The rest of us will follow Jesus. After all, following Jesus is the definition of being the church of Christ.

WHAT MIGHT HAVE HAPPENED THE NIGHT ZACCHAEUS WAS CONVERTED

Now to get back to the narrative of Jesus and Zacchaeus. We are not exactly sure of what happened that evening at Zacchaeus' house before we see Zacchaeus' response. It is clear, however, that Zacchaeus was so moved by the love, presence, and holiness of Jesus that he was profoundly affected. Without a doubt, they ate a meal together, possibly with other friends of Zacchaeus. Over this meal, there would have been plenty of conversation—after all, when you eat a meal with someone, the point is not only to get food in your belly, but to spend time with each other. Having a meal with someone is a profound act of friendship, especially in Jesus' day.[4]

It's likely that in the course of this meal, Zacchaeus talked about his views on life and asked questions about God, and Jesus talked about his views on life and gave answers about God. Knowing Jesus, he didn't pull any punches in regard to what sin was, what was good, and what was evil. It seems that repentance came up, and they talked about God's law.

Given the whole of Jesus' interaction with Zacchaeus, Jesus most likely made clear to Zacchaeus that he was valued as a person, made in the image of God, and that God is merciful to repentant sinners. This falls in line with Jesus' track record in dealing with sinners. God desires reconciliation for those who have gone astray. Look at Zacchaeus' response to Jesus being his friend. Zacchaeus, a very rich man, said this to the Lord: "Behold, Lord, the half of my goods I give to the poor. And if I have defrauded anyone anything, I restore it fourfold" (Luke 19:8). Zacchaeus' response was repentance—a change of mind that leads to a change of actions. Zacchaeus had a change of behavior only after he encountered friendship with Jesus.

IT'S NOT OUR JOB TO CHANGE PEOPLE'S BEHAVIOR

It's not our first responsibility to change the behavior of sinners. It is our first responsibility to introduce our friends to our true and greater friend, Jesus, so they can become friends with him too. And when they become friends with Jesus, their behaviors inevitably change. Very rarely is someone's life change going to be as drastic and immediate as it was with Zacchaeus. But if they meet Jesus the friend of sinners, he is also a good enough friend to change sinners.

> In **#evangelism**, your job is not to get them to behavior modification but to get them to Jesus. Jesus will deal with behavior later.

Here is how Jesus responded to Zacchaeus: he affirmed him with words of salvation by saying, "Today salvation has come to this house, since he is also a son of Abraham" (Luke 19:9). A son of Abraham was sometimes misunderstood to mean that a person was an ethnic Jew, but the term actually refers to a person who comes into a covenant relationship with God by faith, the way Abraham did (Rom 4:11–12). A son of Abraham was someone waiting for God's salvation in the Messiah. The term can also refer to being an ethnic Jew, of course, but in the above passage Jesus is saying that Zacchaeus was declared "just" by faith just like Abraham was. In other words, Zacchaeus was "saved."

Jesus led Zacchaeus to salvation through friendship. Likewise, we lead people to salvation in Jesus most often through friendship as well. Most of your friends are not going to be as notoriously sinful like Zacchaeus; however, because Jesus is not their Lord, their lives will be filled with all sorts of things that make you uncomfortable. They will do and say things that are morally out of bounds with a churchy crowd. They will use language not common in your Bible studies. They won't think twice about gossiping and slandering people. Many times they'll act hatefully and vindictively. They will value many of the wrong things and might be materialistic.

We may be shocked by all of this behavior, but what do we expect? They won't have our morals until they have our Savior. Jesus himself refers to unbelievers as "lost" in the passage we've been covering in this chapter (Luke 19:10). When you are lost, you don't know which direction to go. You are confused, frustrated, irritated, scared, and you often act out because of it. Don't expect your lost friends to act like they are found. They won't, but that is why you are in their lives. Why are we surprised when sinners commit sin? Even when people do have the Savior, they still commit sin and are slow to coming around to living a godly life.

This story in Luke ends with Jesus saying, "The Son of Man came to seek and save the lost" (Luke 19:10). Saving the lost is his mission. Because you belong to Jesus, your mind is joined to his mind, your heart is joined to his heart, and your will is joined to his will. Alongside Jesus, your mission is to seek and save the lost. This means making friends with sinners, like Jesus did.

#Evangelism pushes you out of your comfort zone. Language, culture, raw honesty, & blatant sin will likely make you uncomfortable. Persist.

CHAPTER 2

Putting the Evangel into Evangelism

In the last chapter, we discussed the key to evangelism—a willingness to become a friend to sinners and share the message of salvation. My goal in this chapter is to define the gospel clearly so that we can ingest it ourselves and pass it on to our friends.

If you want to do evangelism, you need to acquaint yourself with the meaning of the word *evangel*, which simply means "gospel." The gospel is the good news about who Jesus is and what Jesus has done. Keep in mind, the gospel is not about what you have achieved by living morally and obeying commandments. (We will get into this in more detail at the end of the book.) Even if your life is a mess, you can help others meet Jesus because you are telling them that Jesus has power to save sinners like you. It's like one beggar telling another beggar where to find food. In fact, God may use your imperfect life to be a platform to preach the gospel. Before we see the gospel as information to share, we must see it as the ground where we stand. Who Jesus is and what he has done are foundational to the Christian life.

THE CLEAR DEFINITION OF "GOSPEL" FROM 1 CORINTHIANS

The Apostle Paul says it best in 1 Corinthians:

> Now I would remind you, brothers, of *the gospel* I preached to you, which you received, in which *you stand*, and by which you are being saved, if you hold fast to the word I preached to you—unless you believed in vain. For I delivered to you as of first importance what I also received: that *Christ died for our sins in accordance with the Scriptures, that he was buried, that he was raised on the third day in accordance with the Scriptures* (1 Cor 15:1–4, emphasis mine).

Standing in the gospel means it's the foundation of the whole Christian life. It means that we remind ourselves of the gospel daily and we're so accustomed to thinking about the gospel for ourselves that it's natural for us to speak to others about it too. Think about it: the gospel is saving you now as you hold this book and breathe air. Let it sink into your soul, let your identity rest in it, hope in it, and fight to trust it. Let it be something you deeply believe and love every day.

EVANGELIZING OURSELVES FIRST

I love what the great evangelist and reformer Martin Luther said about the gospel.

"Most necessary it is, therefore, that we should know this article [the gospel] well, teach it unto others [evangelism], and beat it into their heads continually [discipleship]."[5] That is it! Know it! Experience it! Consume the gospel and then share the gospel. One of the best ways to learn to do evangelism is to first do evangelism on yourself. If we don't experience how the gospel works in our own life, we will have a hard time communicating it to other people. What I mean is that we must learn to preach the gospel to ourselves daily.

Without the gospel, I am a guilt-driven person—I am constantly feeling as if I need to do more and that what I've done is not good enough. During this struggle, I find it very difficult to rest because I am not believing that what Jesus did (the gospel) was enough. Instead, I think I need to add more to the gospel to make myself feel better so I can rest.

For example, I'm writing this on a Saturday morning. Saturday is a day I dedicate to hanging out with my family, enjoying life, and resting. But I also know I need to finish this book, I'm not 100% satisfied with my sermon for Sunday, and people in the church are waiting for me to text or call or email them back. At this moment, I have to tell myself that my righteousness is in Jesus and his works, not mine. Because my righteousness is in Jesus, my sermon does not have to be perfect. My book will get done when it gets done. Those people waiting for me can wait another day so I can rest and be attentive to my family. I don't need their approval because God approves of me, and I also want to be helpful to them because of my calling but not respond to them out of compulsion. I can rest centered in the gospel of God.

In order to do this evangelism of self, you can literally say to yourself, "My rightness is in Jesus! He lived for me. He obeyed the commands of God perfectly on my behalf. He died in my place for my sins. He rose that I might be new and receive the Holy Spirit! My past, present, and future failures or successes no longer define me. Jesus' past, present, and future defines my reality and gives me identity." Jesus will one day heal this broken world and all that makes you weep. You are now a citizen of his kingdom! It is finished! Jesus has done all that you will ever need! God accepts you! God likes you! God loves you! You are now adopted into his family!

Preach the gospel to yourself in joy, pain, and despair. Preach the gospel to yourself even when you sin, when you feel shame, guilt, and doubt, when you succeed, and when you fail. Let the gospel be the home where you live. As the Psalmist preached to himself, "Why so downcast O my soul? Put your hope in God!" (Ps 43:5). When you evangelize yourself first, evangelism with non-Christians doesn't seem so daunting after all. There are two reasons for this.

First, when you preach to yourself regularly, you're confident about the message of the gospel because it resides deep in your own soul.

Second, you have more practice applying the gospel in in every sector of human life. You're regularly "gospeling" yourself in real life. "Gospeling" or evangelizing yourself is what puts flesh and bones on your evangelism with others.

The gospel is not a theory you are delivering but a reality you are wrestling to live in light of. When you're regularly "gospeling" yourself, you'll feel the pain of your own failures and the joy of God's forgiveness. You will identify with doubts and be able to help your friends navigate the pathway to faith. Evangelizing yourself will give authenticity to your evangelism of others.

Let's say you commit *that* sin again. The one that plagues you. For example, you lied. Remind yourself of a verse like this, "If anyone does sin, we have an advocate with the Father, Jesus Christ the righteous" (1 John 2:1). Jesus stands in your place as a reminder before the throne of God that you are forgiven of *that* sin! Jesus prays for you! So instead of beating yourself up internally, preach to yourself, quote truth and Scripture to yourself, and believe it. Your internal talk might be something similar to mine in these times: "You're such a fake. You're supposed to be this Christian, godly person, but you just lied to this person so they might think better of you. You're an imposter, you're a failure. You have no business talking about the gospel, you're not even living out your Christianity." At this moment, you need to tell yourself the verse above and say to yourself, "Yes, I did sin. I am at this moment turning away from that sin and turning to Jesus who died for that sin and rose over all these foolish thoughts in my head." And then, after you have told yourself truth, move on with your day.

PRACTICE EVANGELISM BY EVANGELIZING CHRISTIANS

Another way to practice evangelism is to practice by evangelizing Christians. Yes, Christians need evangelizing too. Through friendships, ministries of the church, family interactions, and wherever we interact with Christians, we should continually preach the gospel to one another. If you read the New Testament carefully, you will find that most of the gospel proclamation outside of the book of Acts is done by Christians to Christians! The New Testament sets out a pattern of evangelizing the church. When you preach the gospel to your Christian friends, they are encouraged by the good news that encourages you. In the process, you get practice for doing evangelism with outsiders. Plus, you have the added benefit of developing a gospel-centered culture in your church, group, family, and friendships.

One day recently, my wife was having a rough morning getting the kids off to school. The kids were distracted, disobedient, and decided on the spur of the moment that they didn't like that kind of pancakes. My wife was hurried, overwhelmed, running behind, and frustrated. She let some of her frustration escape and yelled at the kids a few times. When they went upstairs to get dressed, she confessed to me she felt like a failure and she must be somehow defective as a mother—not just because she yelled, but also because she knew she frequently allowed the behavior of her kids to define her value or worth as a mother.

At moments like these, I am able to remind her that she is made in God's image, and because of the fall, she will never be able to be a perfect mother. The very fact that she recognizes her sin is an evidence of God's grace. All that she needs to do is turn to God in confession and have faith that his works are better and bigger than hers (and, no, she is not ruining her children). It also might be a good idea, I remind her, to apologize to her kids for yelling and to tell them how thankful she is that Jesus died for that sin and he forgives her, and ask for their forgiveness as well. (BONUS: not only has she "gospeled" herself in this, but she has also evangelized her kids.)

Or maybe you have a friend from church who is worried that the bills will not get paid this month. She's afraid her financial situation is going to fall apart and that God is abandoning her. In response, you might preach this gospel bomb from Romans 8:32 to her, "He who did not spare his own Son but gave him up for us all, how will he not also with him graciously give us all things?" Do you see? Evangelizing yourself and other Christians is great practice for doing evangelism.

SIMPLE WAYS TO TALK ABOUT THE GOSPEL

Throughout this book I will explain the gospel in different ways from slightly different angles. But to get us started, let's look at two profound yet simple descriptions of it.

GOD SAVES SINNERS

I love J.I. Packer's description of the Gospel in three words: "God saves sinners."[6] Let's break that down.

God

God is the creator and sustainer of all things. He is perfect, majestic, loving, and just.

Saves

God sent his Son into the world to save the world by living, dying, and rising in the place of sinners to reestablish our relationship with him.

Sinners

As sinners, we break God's law (which is sin), and by doing so, we break God's heart (which is the breaking of our relationship with him.)

THE STORYLINE OF THE BIBLE

Another profound and simple way to look at the gospel is in light of the big storyline of the Bible in four words: Creation, Fall, Redemption, and Re-Creation.

Creation

God makes all that is—seen and unseen—out of nothing, and it is good. Humans are the crowning achievement of this creation because they are made in the image of the creator God.

Fall

Humanity rebels against the creator God by disobeying his command and turns inward in self-reliance. This behavior brings the consequences of sin: death, disease, suffering, war, famine, pain, confusion, and alienation.

Redemption

God promises and sends a Redeemer, Jesus Christ, who reconciles humanity to the creator God. He does this by living the perfect human life, dying a substitutionary death for sinners, and rising from death as the first of a new humanity. Jesus then ascends to heaven and sends God's Spirit to humanity to establish his kingdom in the hearts of his people. This action reestablishes his relationship with them by adopting them into his family.

Re-Creation

Jesus Christ returns to earth to restore creation to God's original intention. All things will be made perfect, sin will be removed, justice will be restored, suffering will cease, tears will be dried, and joy will be fully known. Jesus will rule as king, and we as his people will forever be with God in his home. The kingdom of this world will become the kingdom of our God.

Of course, the gospel is a subject we can't exhaust. It is simple enough for a child to understand, yet so rich that the subject can never be exhausted. Or as Tim Keller says,

"The gospel is not the ABC's of Christianity but the A-Z of Christianity."[7] So there is much more to the gospel than the two examples above, but they should be enough to get us started.[8]

Before we move on, let me say this: in evangelism, our confidence is in the realities of the gospel (Jesus' life, death, and resurrection), not our ability or our methods in communicating it. The Apostle Paul put it this way: "I am not ashamed of the gospel, for it is the power of God for salvation for everyone who believes" (Rom 1:16). The power of God lies within the gospel of God combined with the empowering of the Spirit.

CHAPTER 3

Motives

Now that we've defined "evangelism," it's time to talk about our motives for evangelizing. In order for evangelism to be a part of your life, you need Spirit-empowered motives because directives without vision create apathy. If I just tell you to do evangelism without giving you a vision for why to evangelize, you won't bother to do it. Without motives, the most we can hope for is that you'll feel guilty for not doing it. Evangelism without a gospel-fueled motive will be a huge, joyless, burdensome obligation. So what is the motive?

First, to get the big picture, remember the last couple of chapters that discussed the heaven-sent, gospel-driven motive for befriending sinners. Jesus was a friend of sinners, and being his disciple means following his example. Now we'll focus on the motive for evangelizing in the regular rhythms of day-to-day life. This motive is to see people saved. As the Apostle Paul explained his evangelistic mission, "I have become all things to all people, that by all means I might save some" (1 Cor 9:22).

BROKEN HEARTS FOR LOST PEOPLE

To be a consistent evangelist, we have to stoke the feelings of deep concern for lost souls, and we have to live a lifestyle of evangelism. Evangelism is heart work. Personally, I am not known to have a super emotive personality. But I do feel deeply for people without Christ. I don't want them to be without hope. I can't stand the thought of hoarding salvation for myself without at least trying to bring people into the grace I've received.

Evangelistic work requires a big heart because evangelism is never convenient and is often uncomfortable. You will always encounter opposition from your selfishness (you're going to prefer lounging on the couch with a bag of chips), opposition from the devil (he will try to confuse you and your hearer), and opposition from those who are against the gospel message. If you don't feel a deep love for those without Christ, you will likely stop trying to do evangelism, or avoid it altogether.

The Apostle Paul demonstrates this soul-ache in Romans: "I have great sorrow and unceasing anguish in my heart. For I could wish that I myself were accursed and cut off from Christ for the sake of my brothers, my kinsmen according to the flesh" (Rom 9:2–3). The Apostle Paul is specifically referring to Jews who are without Christ. He wanted people to be saved so badly that he was willing to give up his salvation for the sake of the lost. (Of course, this is impossible, but you can see his heart by this statement.) And all this comes from the guy who wrote the rest of Romans 9 concerning God's election to salvation. For those of you with Reformed or Calvinistic theological convictions (like me), you often love the doctrine of Paul, but not his evangelistic practice.[9]

We must repent of this inconsistent thinking. (If you don't know what "Reformed" or "Calvinistic" means, don't worry about that for now.)

REMEMBER WHAT IT WAS LIKE TO NOT KNOW JESUS

To stoke the fire of concern and love for the lost, take some time to consider your life before Jesus. Remember what it was like to lay your head on the pillow at night and wonder about life. Remember what it was like to numb yourself by keeping yourself busy. It didn't matter what you filled the time with as long as you were busy. Maybe you distracted yourself with good activities like hard work, or damaging pursuits like intoxication. Maybe you filled the void with material things like fast cars, real estate, or entertainment. Or you could have spent all of your time with people—anything to numb the empty feeling you were trying to ignore.

Do you remember what it was like to think about not knowing what awaits you after death? Do you remember what it was like not to have any ultimate purpose, or to feel the endless disappointment of the things of this world? Do you remember knowing down deep that you were made for something great but feeling the pointless, mundane, senseless repetition of life?

If you grew up in church, maybe you can't remember a time when you didn't understand the world and your purpose in life. But you can most likely identify with feeling pointless and flawed when you didn't apply what you believed. Even though you believed in God as a church kid, you can come to a point where you feel the despair. That's what it feels like in the most honest moments of being lost. The point is, we're all lost before meeting Jesus. We all have something in common. We need to be found by our Savior, and fortunately, he's in the saving business.

JESUS' 3 LOST PARABLES (AND THE JOY OF GETTING FOUND)

Jesus told some of his most vivid parables about his heart for those who are lost. In Luke 15, there are three parables that Jesus tells about God's heart for the lost—the lost sheep, the lost coin, and the lost son.

In the parable of the lost sheep, Jesus tells the story of a man who has a hundred sheep and loses one. The shepherd is willing to leave the 99 in the open country to find the one straying sheep. He searches until he finds it, and when he finds it, he rejoices and throws a party. He tells his friends who come to the party, "Rejoice with me, for I have found my sheep that was lost!" (Luke 15:6). This is the way Jesus feels about his lost sheep, and he has sent us to find them. Jesus ends the parable by saying, "There will be more joy in heaven over one sinner who repents than over ninety nine righteous persons who need no repentance" (v. 7). Joy is a motive for evangelism!

In the parable of the lost coin (Luke 15:8–10), a woman loses a valuable coin and diligently cleans her house until it is found. She lights a lamp, moves furniture, sweeps, mops, breaks out the flashlight, and gets her kids on their hands and knees until the coin is found. The parable ends with the same result as the parable of the lost sheep: joy. The woman even throws a party when she finds it. This is how God feels when one of his valued lost children is found (apparently Jesus likes to party). God is inviting us into the joy of his party over lost sinners—he is calling on his people, the church, to share in his joy by gathering his lost kids and inviting them into the family. Unfortunately, we're not very good at this most of the time.

Then there is the parable of the lost son (Luke 15:11–32), often known as the story of the "Prodigal Son." In my opinion this story is the most powerful and vivid of all Jesus' parables.[10] In the story, there is a father and two sons. One of the sons demands his share of his father's estate. The father grants his request, and the son takes the wealth and spends it on parties, women, and possessions until he is broke. Eventually, his money runs out and he finds himself on the street, working for pennies and starving.

He decides he will return to his father and ask to be one of his father's slaves. At least he'd be living in better conditions. He even says, "At least working as a slave would be better than eating with the pigs." But when he returns, he receives the unexpected gift of grace. All along, his father was outside waiting for him to return. When the father sees him, he runs to his son, embraces him, and kisses him. The father gives him the best robe and puts a ring on his finger and shoes on his feet (a way of celebrating the son and showing honor to him). And for the third time in as many parables about the lost, Jesus says the father throws a huge party for the lost son.

THE FATHER'S JOY IN FINDING THE LOST

This is how God feels about the lost. What if we had the heart of the Father? How would that change our lives? We must press in to the heart of the Father in heaven until we feel the same way. Notice that I didn't say "think" the same, but "feel" the same. Are you feeling joy in your Christian life? I have one action step for you. Go hang around some people who don't have the gospel. This will bring you joy because you will remember your own salvation, and what a joy it is to have Christ, and you will be filled with joy to help people discover salvation. Then, of course, like the woman with the lost coin, when they do come to salvation, you will rejoice.

You see, it's one thing to believe sugar is sweet, and another thing to taste it. Our affections have to be stirred if we are going to move toward God's mission. Is your heart broken for lost friends and neighbors? Does it bother you at all? Are you concerned for the outsider? Have you ever wept for lost people, lost cities, or lost friends? Jesus does. Jesus lamented for them (Matt 23:37–39). God told Jonah that he was concerned for them (Jonah 4:11); Paul said he did all things for the sake of them (2 Tim 2:10) and that he became all things to all men that he might save them (1 Cor 9:19–23). God desires all men to be saved (1 Tim 2:4).[11] Do you? If you don't, read Luke 15, thinking about non-Christian people you know, and pray for them until your heart changes. Some of the Puritans used to say, "Pray until you pray." When it comes to evangelism, pray and meditate until you care.

We all get lazy, and often only end up caring about our own interests much of the time. I know I do. But God is calling us to something more. He's on a mission to seek out the lost, and he's given us the privilege to be a part of his work. And when the lost are found, it's cause for a party!

Chapter 4

Evangelistic Praying

*Continue steadfastly in prayer, being watchful in
it with thanksgiving. At the same time, pray also
for us, that God may open to us a door for the
word, to declare the mystery of Christ.*

Col 4:2–3a

About 5 years ago, my family moved into the house where we are currently living. Before we moved in, I spent time prayer-walking our neighborhood, asking God to let us find a house in this neighborhood that will have neighbors he is calling into his kingdom. We got the house, and I fully expected that my neighbors would be coming to Christ over the course of the years that we lived there. I believed this because it is the kind of prayer that is in line with God's will.

Within a couple of months, a woman named Tracy moved in next door. We immediately began praying for her. The following few months, we had many interactions with her in the yard. My wife, Rachael, enjoyed Tracy's company and would frequently go over and chitchat with her. She began to learn the story of Tracy's life and the events that led her to move into the house. Tracy also very much liked our dog, Lady.

One day in mid-December, while she was away at work, Tracy's home was broken into and burglarized. She was very distraught, and Rachael went over to her house. After listening and sitting with her awhile, Rachael asked Tracy if she could pray for her. She said, "Yes," and Rachael prayed. This one act of praying changed the dynamics of the relationship they would have in the future. Their relationship became much more personal, and an element of mutual trust grew that hadn't been there before. Something happened to the souls of these two women that paved the way for many future gospel conversations. We continued to pray for Tracy and actually began sharing custody of our dog, Lady, with her. She had weekend visitation.

After a dozen or so gospel conversations, Tracy started coming to church with us. Four years of praying and talking to her about the gospel were beginning to have an effect. The relationship my wife built with Tracy began to flourish, and it came to a point where it was natural for her to attend church with us, and she even felt comfortable to sit with us almost every week. Thankfully, I can say that in the last few months she's been converted to Christ, and now she wants to get baptized in light of her commitment to Jesus. What Tracy didn't know is that before she moved in, we prayed for her; we prayed for her regularly during those four years, and we are still praying for her now.

PRAYER: THE FORCE AND FUEL OF EVANGELISM

I say all this to point out that we simply need to be in prayer for those around us who need God. We need to be spiritually fueled up so we can see opportunities when they present themselves. Evangelistic prayer is talking to God about the people in your life you're evangelizing. Prayer is the force and fuel of evangelism because prayer is an expression of our dependence on God. Prayer is admitting that God is God, and you are in need of him. This is certainly true in evangelism. You need God to show up and do the God-stuff that only he can do.

Think about it theologically. You need God to give you courage (Acts 4). You need God to give you the right words (Matt 10:16–18). You need God to direct you to the right people (John 6:65). You need God to open hearts (Acts 16:14). You need God to keep demonic activity at bay so that the word is not snatched from people's hearts (Matt 13:19).

In other words, if you do not pray, you are not likely to see people come to Jesus. Pray like God has elected the people he desires to save (1 Pet 1:1). Pray because God is more eager to save them than you are. Pray with joy because the results of evangelism are up to God. Somebody likely prayed for you to come into the kingdom. Evangelism works by the God of heaven being moved by the prayers of his people as his people proclaim his gospel.

GRANDMA PRAYED FOR ME. WHO PRAYED FOR YOU?

Those of us who don't have a memory of always being a Christian can probably remember the people praying for us—like my grandma Rosalie. She prayed for me for years as I wandered; from what I understand, she rarely missed a day of praying for me. She pleaded with God to save me and override my rebellious will. She prayed that I'd have an open heart to the gospel. But as she labored in prayer, it seemed I moved further into darkness and sin.

What she could not have known is that during those years I quietly considered God. I considered him when relationships fell apart and I felt lonely, and I prayed to God in my sadness or fear. One time, I was doing work crew for a previous drug arrest and conviction. This was my third or fourth time on work crew, and they had never done a drug test. That morning, they were doing a series of eye tests to determine if anyone was high. I was in line and extremely high off of multiple drugs and had been up all night. I knew I was done for, and this would mean jail time. So I prayed, "God if you get me out of this one, I promise I will dedicate the rest of my life to serving and following you. Please rescue me. I don't deserve for you to save me from this, but I'm asking anyway." I passed that drug test and would become a Christian about six months later.

I also prayed in despair during these times, longing for deliverance from loneliness. I loathed my inadequacies, hated my dark heart, and admired the Savior from a distance. I would have never admitted it then, but God was working. In fact, every movement of my life demonstrated the opposite of progress toward faith and belief, but God's Spirit was moving below the surface. I finally caved under the weight of free grace; captivated by Jesus Christ, I was no match for his love and power. Grandma prayed, and God in heaven moved.

Since becoming a Christian, and eventually a pastor, dozens of people have told me they prayed for my conversion. Prayer is a force to be reckoned with because God is on the receiving end of the communication, and God uses our prayers in his sovereign rule to save sinners. Grandma not only prayed for me, but she prayed for all my cousins as well. As I sit to write this, all but one of us walks with Jesus. I don't doubt that the other will cave under the weight of the Spirit-driven prayers of Grandma. Evangelism and prayer change lives.

As I reflect on grandma Rosalie's prayers for me, I'm reminded that one of the best ways to prepare ourselves for evangelism is by praying. Pray for the specific people in your life outside of Christ. Pray for their hearts to be opened and lives to be invaded by God.

PRAY FOR SPECIFIC PEOPLE

Involve other Christians as you pray for those you evangelize. Share the names of people you're praying for with your small group Bible study, at church, with your family, or among friends. I also tell the people I am evangelizing that I am praying for them. They usually appreciate that and thank me. I ask them how I can pray for them, and sometimes they call or text me with prayer requests.

Don't get intimidated by prayer for people. It's really not complicated. Here's an example. One of my friends is having a tough time right now. His marriage is falling apart, so I pray that our conversations about Jesus' love for the church and how that relates to marriage will make sense to him. My hope is that he can understand the gospel and save his marriage.

Another friend is struggling with substance abuse and the brokenness of his past. He struggles to forgive himself because he thinks he needs to atone for his sins. I pray that the substitutionary sacrifice of Christ will make sense to him so that he can be free from that burden.

Another neighbor friend of mine reads new age books and thinks we are all little "christs." I pray he'll recognize he doesn't have the answer to salvation within his own heart, but that salvation is in Jesus, outside of his personal experience.

I have another friend named Dave. I haven't talked to him about anything but beer, kids, and our neighborhood. But I have a prayer that I pray for him that goes like this: "Save Dave!" The point is, pray for people you desire to reach.

PRAY AFTER YOUR CONVERSATIONS

It's also important to pray after evangelistic conversations. Pray that your friend would consider what was said. Pray that God would internally deconstruct their roadblocks. Pray that the devil wouldn't influence their thinking. Pray there would be a chance for future conversations. Prayer causes us to do evangelism in a God-centered, Spirit-dependent, Spirit-empowered way. We are not relying on human ingenuity but on God who raised Christ from the dead.

Remember, evangelism isn't sales or persuasion; evangelism is raising the dead! And only God can do that, so we must pray.

Chapter 5

How to Talk to People about the Gospel

PEOPLE ARE MORE THAN PROJECTS

We sometimes fail in evangelism because people can detect when we see them as a project, rather than a person. You see, we can aim to be friends of sinners. We might have our definition of the gospel straight and be praying for the gospel conversations to come. But if people perceive we have an agenda that doesn't have anything to do with a desire for friendship with them, they'll notice.

You have to ask yourself this question: do I want to lead this person to Christ so that I can feel better about myself and tell my Christian friends about it, or do I want to lead this person to Christ because I respect and love them and want them to experience God's goodness? Evangelism can become a sort of transaction where we get something out of the lost person—like holiness points with God. If getting another notch on your belt is your motivation for evangelism, you will fail. People will see right through it, and evangelism will become a joyless chore.

The proper motivation for evangelism is that we are "compelled by the love of Christ" (2 Cor 5:14). He has loved us, and at great cost to himself, he has sought us out. So we bring the news of his grace to others. Our joy is to communicate this gospel, the good news of a perfect Savior who died in the place of sinners, rose again from the dead, and will one day return. We get to tell people this news, and as we do, the Apostle Paul gives us insight into how to talk to people about this gospel. Paul conceptually builds out evangelism along the lines of friendship and relationship.

THE BEST RELATIONAL EVANGELISM VERSES IN THE BIBLE

Evangelism is inherently relational. You, a relational being, speak to another relational being about a relational gospel given by a relational God. The best instruction on relational evangelism I know of in the Bible is in Colossians 4:5–6. Here the Apostle Paul instructs us,

> Walk in wisdom toward outsiders, making the best use of the time. Let your speech always be gracious, seasoned with salt, so that you may know how you ought to answer each person.

Notice that the whole passage pivots on the two words "toward outsiders." Paul is addressing how to speak to those outside the faith, to those who don't yet know Jesus. He does not mean in any way that unbelievers are to be avoided or that they are not welcome. In fact, the entire passage is an instruction on how to make outsiders *insiders*. This is what evangelism is all about: helping those outside the grace of God come inside the grace of God.

I see five evangelistically relational exhortations in these two verses to guide us into practical evangelism:

- Be wise
- Be present
- Be gracious
- Be interesting
- Be interested

Let's walk through this passage and learn how to talk to outsiders about Jesus.

1. BE WISE

"Conduct yourselves wisely . . ." Colossians 4:5

Wisdom is about living with skill. In this passage, the Apostle is instructing us to live (walk) with wisdom in the way we interact with those outside the faith. You might call this missional or evangelistic skill. Many approaches to evangelism completely ignore the call to wisdom.

For example, imagine an angry street corner preacher holding a sign confronting cultural values. If you stop to talk to one of these guys, you can bet the conversation will focus on hell and damnation.

Or think about the cult member on a mission to litter a neighborhood or parking lot with tracts or to carry out a quota of door-to-door cold calls. And of course there's always the bait-and-switch event like the Christian rock concert. Once you have everyone there for the entertainment, a preacher arrives on stage and, to everyone's dismay, explains the four spiritual laws. And you thought it was a rock concert!

I'm not saying that these methods have never worked or that they never work today. But each approach probably lacks wisdom in a secular society. If you don't believe me, just ask non-Christians about their impressions of Christians. You'll quickly find that many evangelistic methods reinforce these unfortunate caricatures of Christianity.

Zeal, Wisdom, and a Cat Named "Dog"

When I was a kid we had a cat named "Dog" who loved to chase birds. Dog was as zealous as any cat ever was about birds, but he had a really bad method. He would sleep on top of the birdhouse in anticipation. I guess he figured he'd "hit them where they live." Of course, the birds avoided the birdhouse because Dog just wanted to eat them. Dog had all the zeal needed to catch birds, but none of the hunting wisdom. Likewise, many would-be evangelists have plenty of zeal to see people saved, but lack missionary wisdom.

Most of the evangelistic fruit that I have seen comes from building friendships and sharing my life with others, which eventually translates into sharing my faith. In other words, living with missionary wisdom is living in skillful, intentional friendships with outsiders. In part, this means that I don't make it a goal to attack an unbeliever's values. I may eventually challenge them, but I don't expect Christian behavior or belief from an unbeliever. They're still living in the construct of the world they created, or that has been created for them by the world—the culture, humanistic thinking, and the devil. I don't feel the need to be the theological police with them, but instead I strive to understand where they're coming from whether their belief is false or not. I might have a friend tell me he believes all roads lead to God and that all religions are talking about the same thing. I might listen, affirm that I understand what he is talking about and why he came to that conclusion, but then I might also ask him where he got the knowledge that all roads lead to God. I would ask him, "what if someone's road included the harm of other people? Does that road also lead to God?" I would ask him if he can understand why I believe that there are invalid roads. But if he gets the sense that I've got an agenda, it shows that I don't have wisdom like the cat named "Dog" who's waiting around for that easy catch.

Be Ready to Point Out the Good in Others

Sometimes when I am hanging out with non-Christians, they want to make jokes that de-humanize women. They might be getting drunk while we are talking, and they might use language that I would not consider appropriate. I am careful to not join them in sin. Without shaming them and without a self-righteous announcement, I strive to obey God's commands. I don't feel the need at that moment to point out everything that they are doing wrong, but instead I try to catch them doing right or believing right.

For example, when my friend says to me that he really wants to make sure that his kids grow up knowing that their dad loves them and is interested in them, I might tell him that is exactly what the Bible says to fathers. When a neighbor tells me they are intentional about riding their bike to work and recycling because they care about the earth, I might tell her that Genesis 1 and 2 give humanity a mandate from God to care about the earth and the Scripture agrees with her passion for environmentalism. When I say these things to these people, I am showing them that Christianity holds within it many things that they already believe.

When they say or do something that does line up with truth, I affirm it. Encourage them, serve them, joke around with them, be concerned about what they are concerned about, and enjoy them as a human being. Look for the evidences of the image of God in them and the wisdom they have, and affirm it when you see it.

Non-Believers Have Wisdom Too (Tell Them You Notice)

In the Bible, wisdom is about living with godly skill. As Proverbs 9:10 explains, "The Fear of the Lord is the beginning of wisdom." Much of the book of Proverbs deals with how to have healthy relationships. The book of Proverbs gives instruction on boundaries, conflict, loyalty, marriage, parenting, money, friendship, and many other life issues from a God-centered perspective. Wisdom is often the bridge between outsiders and insiders.

My non-Christian friends don't identify with my faith in Christ yet, but they really appreciate what Scripture says about how to navigate their relationships. The book of Proverbs is a pre-evangelistic gold mine. You can use this wisdom to help your friends before you share the gospel with them. Sometimes this takes a while.

Being wise is also about *how* you interact with people. Are you using the relational skills that the book of Proverbs teaches? Are you humble, winsome, loving, content, generous, and filled with the knowledge of God? None of us do this perfectly, of course. In fact, admitting your weakness and struggle and regularly asking forgiveness and taking ownership of mistakes is part of what will make you winsome and wise. Nobody likes a perfectionist. Outsiders often call that person a hypocrite. They can see right through it. People understand needs and grief and guilt and feelings of inadequacy. They understand this brokenness and they can see yours. You might as well be real about it. Walking in wisdom is the pathway to gospel conversations.

2. BE PRESENT

"... making the best use of the time ..."
Colossians 4:5

Missional living involves active use of time. Time is a gift that we only have so much of. Time will pass us quickly if we are not present in it. To be present is to give the whole of your person to someone in that exact moment. You are giving the physical elements and mental elements of yourself to them by physical touch, making eye contact, intently listening, verbally responding, and using body language like nodding your head. You are also giving your mental capabilities to them. You might do this by repeating back to them what they said in a slightly different way, showing that you understand or agree with them verbally when you can. By being present, you are also giving your heart to them. When they show any kind of emotion, anger, frustration, sadness, or joy, you are appropriately responding with emotion as well. You're not faking it, but you are feeling with them. This what I mean by "being present." When the Apostle Paul says, "make use of the time," he's pointing out that we only have so much time with those outside the faith. Think about the business of your own life. Between your spouse, kids, parents, family, local church, work, sleep and personal time, your time with non-Christians is limited. Make good use of that time. Don't waste it. Be present when they are present.

#Evangelism happens on their time, not your time.

First, make time to seek out relationships with outsiders. Second, make time to develop relationships with outsiders. One of the biggest roadblocks to evangelism is laziness. You will actually need to go out and do it. Rather than approaching evangelism as another checklist item, make it a part of the natural rhythms of your life. Instead of adding something to your schedule, develop these relationships as you go. The command in the Great Commission is to go and make disciples (Matt 28:18–20). It could also be translated, "As you go . . . make disciples." In other words, as you are living in the rhythms of your life, be intentional to make disciples of people who are not currently disciples. This is using your time wisely in being present with those you encounter.

Let's get practical. Here are some ways to be present with unbelievers.

Be Neighborly

Chances are, you have neighbors, so act like one. Make the effort to go meet them. Offer to help them with yard work, hang out outside until you get in conversations, take walks in your neighborhood, or throw a block party. With neighbors, take the long-term approach of developing a good neighborly reputation in the neighborhood. Chances are, your neighbors are talking. You are working to build friendships in the neighborhood, so be careful how you interact. Avoid unnecessary conflict, and be a good neighbor. Let me give you an example of a conflict with a neighbor I didn't handle very well, but by God's grace we have recovered the situation.

The long and the short of it is that I accidentally built a fence on my property line that went 1–2 inches into a neighbor's property line. Keep in mind that this 1 or 2 inches is on the back side of his house that he never uses and oddly enough his property line goes a few inches into my concrete driveway. I told my neighbor that I was going to build a fence. He told me he wanted me to wait to have a surveyor to come and determine the property. I didn't think it was an issue because the fence was getting built directly on top of my driveway. I told him it wouldn't be a problem, and I had the fence built. As it turns out, the surveyor came and affirmed that my fence and driveway extended a few inches into his property.

My neighbor was furious. When I met with him, he was visibly shaking with anger. At that moment, I had a decision to make: I could either make my case regarding the concrete driveway, the couple of inches, the fact that it's an old neighborhood and property lines have been confused, and that after all, we are only talking about a couple of inches here. But instead, by God's grace, I didn't say those things. Instead I said, "I was wrong. I should've waited. I'll do whatever we need to do to make this right. Will you please forgive me?" When I said, "Will you forgive me?" He was literally speechless. While he didn't grant forgiveness, he did work with me on a solution that allowed us to keep the fence up. I probably had a case to make and could have engaged him legally. But, in the end, I decided that the relationship with him and the other neighbors was far more important. Not to mention, they all know that I am a pastor at the church a half-mile from the house.

Go To A Regular "Spot"

Get out of the house and go to coffee shops, pubs, restaurants, barbershops, salons, a golf course, the park, the court or the gym. Get to know the staff and customers, tip well, be friendly, ask people about themselves, and be available to talk. I have seen amazing fruit by just going to my favorite spots and doing my favorite hobbies. I am striving to build a reputation as the biggest tipper and most easy-to-please customer at these places so that when a gospel conversation comes up, or they realize that I am a Christian pastor, I will have a platform to speak from.

Go To Work

Work hard and keep a good attitude. Show up to your shift on time, be reasonable in conflict, don't engage in gossip, and be relationally available to people. Before I was a pastor, I had dozens of opportunities to talk about Christ, pray for people, and take people from work to church. When you go to work, pray and ask the Spirit to fill you with himself, and be available to serve people. Don't be a Bible thumper, don't get self-righteous, and don't get caught up in office drama. Over time, God will use you. He has you there for a reason—don't get discouraged. Often, the same people who mock your faith will end up asking for prayer, and some will meet Jesus. When I worked at UPS, I was one of two Christians out of 200 employees. When we were in a group working together, many of the employees would tease me about my faith, but when I got alone with any one of them, they often asked me about God, church, Jesus, or my story. Some of them even came to me asking for prayer at tough times in their life.

Get Involved In The Community

Kid's sports and activities, clean-up efforts, clubs, volunteer organizations, support groups, book clubs, or sports teams—these group activities allow you to develop friendships around common goals or interests without awkwardness.

Once you've developed the above ways to connect with unbelievers, you will need to develop relationships with these people. This is usually a slow process. Most of the people I currently evangelize have been my friends for months or years. Many of them have been to my home, and I've been to theirs. Then there are others whom I talk to here and there whenever I happen to see them. With some, I have in-depth conversations about faith, religion, and the gospel; with others, I've only mentioned Christ in the midst of everyday conversation. And with some of these people, I have never mentioned Christ. They don't know I'm a Christian, and I haven't explained the gospel. But my plan is to get there. It's all part of the process. Whatever the depth of relationship, just make sure you use the time well.

Here's the main thing about using time well with unbelievers: be present with them. Make an impression. Make your time together about them, not you or your "mission" to get them saved, or to score points with God. Here's the most important thing: listen. I am convinced that listening to others well is one of the most important skills for evangelism. We tend to think the skill of speaking is what's important. But it's not the most important. If you listen well, you'll know how to move forward in conversation with them. Most people desperately want a listening presence in their life. When two friends are present and in the moment with one another, a meaningful interaction can take place. When you're focused this way in your relationships, you won't default to "project mentality." You'll see others as they are, real people with souls and stories. She is a person who needs God just like you, even though she doesn't know it.

> **#Evangelism** is almost never convenient.

3. BE GRACIOUS

> **"Let your speech always be gracious, seasoned with salt . . ." Colossians 4:6**

Eventually, it will be time to share the gospel of grace, so communicate it *graciously*. Let your heart be so filled with the love Jesus has for you that when you teach others about his love they sense it in you.

Be kind and friendly. Don't get frustrated if they argue or disagree. As the Apostle Peter says, "Always be prepared to make a defense to anyone who asks you for a reason for the hope that is in you; yet do it with *gentleness and respect*" (1 Pet 3:15, emphasis mine). Gentleness and respect are key to any relationship, but especially in a situation where you are confronting a person's core beliefs. If they have real questions about Christianity, see it as an opportunity to instruct rather than an argument to deconstruct. God can use someone's contentions with Christianity and the gospel as the very thing that brings him or her back to Jesus. Keep in mind that the people who usually are the most contentious are wrestling with the concepts. So, be gracious. They just need time and someone to help them talk things through, answer questions, and spur them on to think about the things of God. There's no reason to be threatened by their pushback. Of course they will struggle. Think about it—you are telling them their life is not good enough to earn God's approval and they need a Savior who wants control of their life. These are not small things! Be gracious and let the Holy Spirit do his work. When God draws someone, nothing can stop him—have patience, have confidence, and by all means, be gracious! Answer their questions, talk about their issues, but keep bringing them back to Jesus.

I try to keep the conversation focused on the issue we're discussing instead of taking up a "me versus them" attitude in the conversation. Also, realize most unbelievers don't accept the Bible as an authoritative book, so it's best to approach conversation in a non-argumentative way. I do this by prefacing what I say with general statements like "from a Christian perspective," or "Jesus said," or "the Apostles taught," or the "Jewish Scriptures teach us." This seems to be much more helpful than telling them that they are wrong or making them feel stupid in how you respond to them.

Don't forget that you also have a lot to learn from your unbelieving friends, and they can teach you many things about life, relationships, and happiness. When you do learn from them, make sure to thank them for the example they have set.

Remember, you are trying to win a person not a debate. Debates are about winning arguments; relationships are about winning people. Relationships require give and take, time, and attention. Relationships require emotional investment.

You will also need to be gracious with other religious and moral views. If those you are evangelizing feel you lack respect for them or their tradition, they won't listen to yours. Sympathize with their worldview to the degree that you can. Atheists and people of other religions are smart people too. These folks have good reasons and logic for why they believe what they believe. Remember that, given their set of circumstances, background, and information, you might believe similar things. Also, remember that, apart from the Spirit of God opening your eyes to the gospel, you would be just as lost. Humility is key. Graced people grace people.

4. BE INTERESTING

> **"Let your speech always be gracious, seasoned with salt..." Colossians 4:6**

Paul also instructs us that our speech should be "seasoned with salt." That means, add some flavor to your conversation. We use salt on food to bring out the flavor of the food, and likewise, we use salt within our gospel conversations to bring out the flavor of the gospel. Be yourself, and let your personality come out. If you're smart, humbly reference research from a textbook. If you're winsome, persuade someone with your kindness. If you're funny, tell a joke. If you're an extrovert, let your excitement win them over.

A word to the introverts out there: effective evangelism is not bound to a personality type. There are as many types of evangelists as there are people. You don't need to be an outgoing extrovert to evangelize well. My friends know I'm an introverted guy. I'm terrible at small talk and typically engage conversations away from the action whenever I'm at a party. God uses you, not some idealized version of you. Extroversion is no better than introversion, and there are flawed versions of both relational styles. God will use you in all your strength, weakness, quirks, flaws, and brokenness. My wife is an outgoing social butterfly who networks with dozens of people at a time. By doing this she gets into gospel conversations on a regular basis. I am more of a quiet, methodical, one conversation at a time kind of guy. Both of us see evangelistic fruit.

The truth is, every person is interesting because they're unique. You will be an effective evangelist when you are you. God made you the way you are, and only you can reach the people God has designed you to reach. Don't try to be someone else. Be a Spirit-filled you. People will love it, and if not, don't worry about it; if they belong to God, someone else will reach them.

5. BE INTERESTED

> " . . . so that you may know how you ought
> to answer each person." Colossians 4:6

Paul instructs us to "answer each person." Of course, each person has different questions, issues, and struggles. Those we meet come from different cultures, races and life-stages. This is why canned gospel presentations rarely work. If we engage others with this canned approach, they're going to see right through it. They'll be able to tell that they're just a project to you, not a person to be in relationship with. Be interested, and let the Holy Spirit fill you and open the doors to talk about the gospel. Respond to each person individually. Like I said previously, make the conversation about them. Get to know them, their aspirations, dreams, disappointments, and questions. I do this by asking lots of questions about who they are and what's going on in their life. Most people love to talk about themselves and their interests. What I've found is that people really want to be heard and understood, and I love learning about people. Evangelism is a lot about listening, curiosity, and being interested.

Staying interested is also the best way to know how to get to Jesus in conversation with the person. You will get a sense for who they are, what they feel, and what they need. And when the opportunity comes, sharing the news of Jesus will come naturally. When spiritual conversation comes up, get them to Jesus, and be sure that it's the gospel that you are talking about. Answer questions, wrestle with issues, but keep bringing them back to Jesus. I'm not saying you should be robotic; simply talk to people about the gospel in a way that respects and honors their personhood (they are not a project). You don't need to force it. Sometimes you will get in a few words pointing to Jesus. Other times it will lead to hours of deep spiritual conversation.

Chapter 6

Moving from Common Grace to Special Grace

I n the previous chapter we talked about how to engage people with the gospel. We discussed what it is to be wise in our relationships and to make the best use of time evangelizing others—what it is to be present, interested and gracious with them. Now we'll look at another aspect of commonality we can find with unbelievers in order to build relational bridges. And this is through common graces we all experience. Throughout the history of the church, theologians often talk about God's grace as found in the Bible in two helpful categories: common grace and special grace.

DEFINING THE TERMS

Common Grace

God gives common grace to all people. Common graces are essentials like food, rain, air, clothing, natural resources, love, friendships, and family. But common graces are also parts of life that are not essential, like the enjoyment of sports, art, music, film, coffee, beer, bacon, ice cream, fashion, or your kids' toys.

Special Grace

God's special grace doesn't necessarily come to mankind in general. God's special graces are things like the Bible, the gospel found in the revelation in Jesus Christ and the giving of the Holy Spirit.

When we evangelize, one of the most practical and effective things we can do is first connect with people based on God's common graces and move people toward God's special graces. In between, there is usually a relational bridge that I will explain below.

COMMON GRACE AND EVANGELISM

The beautiful thing about God's common grace is that it is familiar to everyone, whether that person is a Christian or not. These common graces are one of the major things we can all relate to and enjoy. They serve as opportunities to make significant connections with people outside the faith, while enjoying something we already love. Let me give you some examples.

Babies. Kids are a common grace. My wife has had dozens of meaningful evangelistic conversations with women at our kids' schools because they connect over the common grace of motherhood. Likewise, I've connected with several of the dads. I've had significant gospel conversations with many of them, and some of them have come to church. This is how it works: my wife takes the kids to school and picks them up every day. There are dozens of other parents doing the same. Their kids often have the same classes as mine. When you see someone day after day, eventually you get into conversations. In this environment, everyone has kids in common, and every parent loves to talk about his or her kids. Eventually, some of these conversations lead to people sharing about other aspects of their life, but the initial connection was over a common grace—kids, babies, growing up, parenthood, bedtime routines, homework, braces, you name it.

George, one of the pastors at our church, is an avid brewer of fine beers, something I consider to be a common grace. George connects with men from all over our city also interested in homebrewing. They share recipes and strategies, and over time, he has built significant friendships with people who don't go to church.

Another friend of mine is an avid fisherman. He connects with many of the best fishermen in our area and is highly respected in that community. He spends a couple days a week with non-Christian guys bonding over the common grace of fishing. Through this common grace, he has built all sorts of friendships and connections he wouldn't have otherwise.

Here's another example. Every year, our church partners with over 60 local businesses and hundreds of local artists to put on the "Midtown Art Walk" just outside of downtown Reno. The purpose of this art walk is to help revitalize the city by giving exposure to artists, entrepreneurs, and local businesses. We're partnering mostly with non-Christians and rallying around the common grace of strengthening the city. When we do this art walk, it brings cultural revitalization to the neighborhood in the vicinity of our church building. Year after year we've made connections with hundreds of people in our city around this common grace.

BRIDGING THE RELATIONAL GAP

This is the way it usually works. You make connections with people over common graces, and as friendships develop, eventually they open up and share their lives with you. Before you know it, you're walking together as friends. Maybe they start opening up to you about their struggling marriage, and you open up to them about your own struggles. Before you know it, you are applying a biblical worldview and gospel applications to their marriage.

Let me give you an example. A couple weeks ago, I was talking to a non-Christian friend with serious marriage problems. For a long time I just listened, heard him out, and did my best to sympathize with his pain and struggle. I didn't correct him or try to give him any advice. I was just there for him. Eventually, he asked me what I thought he should do. This gave me the opportunity to talk about different approaches to marriage. One is based on score keeping, and the other is based on unmerited love. I explained the difference between a grace-based and works-based marriage. I told him that when you have a works-based marriage, you always keep score, trying to one-up your spouse. You want to make sure they pay for the wrongs they have done and that you get what is owed to you. In a grace-based relationship, the relationship isn't based on performance but free, unmerited love. He had never heard anything like this, and it went against everything he had ever learned in his life. This even went against what his marriage therapist and 12-step program had taught him. He told me that this was a new concept he had never heard of before, but that if his marriage was ever going to work, something like this was the only hope. This takes us to special grace.

GOD'S SPECIAL GRACE

This is where God's special grace comes in. Though my friend and I had hung out a dozen times in various different circumstances, this was the first time I explained the gospel to him from beginning to end. We talked about human sin and how God is moved with one-way love, or as one author stated, "Grace is love that is coming at you that has nothing to do with you."[12] Grace is unmerited and free from God to us. I explained to him that God gave us this grace through Jesus. Jesus became human, lived for us, died for us, rose for us, sent the Spirit to us, and will come back for us. I explained that we do nothing at all to earn his salvation or love.

He didn't become a Christian over that meal, but he told me our conversation was one of the best things he had ever heard. He wondered why the gospel had never been explained to him that way growing up in the Roman Catholic Church. He said that if his marriage was going to somehow work out, he'd have to start with grace because they had both done too much to each other to ever go the way of works. It would have to start over with grace.

What I did was apply special graces to his life in the midst of our conversation. I told him of the special grace of God's revelation in the Bible, the special grace of God's Son, and the special grace of God's gospel. These are things that he did not have access to as a human, but by applying special grace to him, which is evangelism, I made him aware of these graces, which could possibly, in turn, lead him to the knowledge of his need for these graces.

FINDING THE RELATIONAL BRIDGE TO SPECIAL GRACE CONVERSATIONS

Here's where the relational bridge comes in. That conversation was possible because we first connected over the common grace of being entrepreneurs. He'd started several successful restaurants, and I'd started several churches. Our friendship began with me learning from him about entrepreneurship. Our relationship had a movement over the bridge of common grace. We bonded over a shared interest, and the conversation took shape over time. Once there was mutual trust, he felt free to share about his personal life and our shared common grace allowed for a conversation of special grace.

Connect with people over the common graces in your life—things that you love and are already doing. Make friends, be present, and let God open the door to share the gospel. When he opens that door, walk through it. Sometimes it's just that easy.

CHAPTER 7

Don't Get Weird

*We've all been there, the conversation is
going fine—and then somehow, some way
the conversation turns to Jesus.*

When I worked at UPS, I was put on a special
project in the back of the warehouse with my co-
worker, Josh. We had a four-hour shift together
on the same job. I'm pretty sure the conversation just started
with usual small talk about sports and music and common
interests. Throughout the conversation, he revealed to me
that his girlfriend was breaking up with him and that he was
broken-hearted and didn't know what to do next. Then he flat-
out asked me about God. At this point, I had been a Christian
about a year. I said something to him about being saved. He
said something like, "What do I need to do to be saved?" Even
though the guy had never read the Bible before, he was in need
and knew he needed more than what he had.

Unfortunately, that was the moment I got weird. In the previous three hours of conversation, I had been relaxed, we had been laughing and enjoying one another's company. But, when it came time to preach the greatest news in the world to my friend who had asked for it, the best I could say was, "God's plan of salvation." He then, of course, said, "What is God's plan of salvation?" I got cotton-mouthed. I'm pretty sure I was blushing, and I started stuttering and stumbled through some kind of Christan-ese gospel presentation. He developed a very confused look on his face and then changed the subject.

The situation reminded me of Acts 16:30, when the jailer asks Paul, "What must I do to be saved?" However, unlike Paul, I was unprepared for the conversation and ended up missing a great opportunity. If I didn't believe in the sovereignty of God, I would be confident that it was my fault that Josh didn't understand the gospel that day because I got really weird and wasn't prepared to talk to someone about Christ on the spot like that.

THE PROBLEM (WHEN OUR DEMEANOR BETRAYS OUR MESSAGE)

While the conversation was on the topic of golf, business strategy, or your kids' school play, you were fine, you were laughing, you were comfortable, you were yourself, and you were having fun. But when conversation turned to Jesus, you got weird. You got tongue-tied and cotton-mouthed. You started breathing heavily; you got very serious and relationally cold. Any hint of joy was gone from your demeanor as you began to talk to them about the Greatest News Ever.

Do you see the contradiction? When talking about anything else (like fishing, business, or the school play), you're fine. You're relaxed. But when you talk about the gospel, your demeanor betrays your message. Your friends think it's weird when you get weird. Relax. Trust God. Breathe. And then talk about the gospel like you talk about other things, naturally.

EVANGELISM ISN'T A SALES PITCH

Some of the tension comes from the idea that you're making a sales pitch, requiring you to close the deal. When you talk about sports or family, this tension is not there. Let me put your mind at ease. Evangelism is not sales. You are not closing deals and gathering commissions for heaven. Jesus has already supplied all that you need for salvation. On the cross he cried out "It is finished" and "paid in full." Your salvation is secure, and any person you lead to Christ will do so because of what Jesus has done, not because of what you do or how well you do it.

IT'S NOT ALL DEPENDENT ON YOU

The other reason you can chill is that the salvation of souls is not dependent upon your evangelistic execution. You speak the message, you develop the relationship, but it is ultimately the Spirit of God who brings a person to salvation. Consider how Lydia, the non-Christian, wealthy woman from Asia, came to salvation under the evangelism of Apostle Paul. "The Lord opened her heart to pay attention to what was said by Paul" (Acts 16:14).

This passage is a good reminder that we are not the ones ultimately responsible for results in evangelism. In the plan of

God, the evangelist is the means of evangelism, but not the cause of its effectiveness. Here's another example. When Paul and Barnabas evangelized in Antioch of Pisidia, not everyone believed, but some did. And these verses tell us why: "And when the Gentiles heard this, they began rejoicing and glorifying the word of the Lord, and *as many as were appointed to eternal life believed.* And the word of the Lord was spreading throughout the whole region" (Acts 13:48, emphasis mine). Results are God's business; evangelism is our business. So don't get weird.

OUR WEIRDNESS AND BEING ASHAMED OF THE GOSPEL

Another reason we get weird is that, if we admit it, we get ashamed of the gospel. Just think about it for a moment. We believe that there is a forever-existing God who spoke the universe into existence and created humans in his likeness. We also believe that the first humans disobeyed this God because a talking snake tricked them. We believe that this God did many miracles throughout history and then eventually became a human, lived in obscurity for 30 years, then spent three years traveling around the Middle East as a homeless preacher, walking on water, multiplying food, healing people, and preaching the greatest sermons ever preached. We believe that he proceeded to give himself up to die like a common criminal, and that when he died, it canceled out all our sins, and that when he lived, he lived to give us a perfect record for our life. Here's another crazy part, we believe that dead guy rose again from the dead, told his followers to go into the world and preach about his resurrection, and then he flew up into heaven and disappeared into the clouds. Oh, and by the way, he's coming back to rule the whole earth. On the surface, these beliefs sound like foolishness. And they are! "For the word of the cross is folly to those who are perishing, but to us who are being saved it is the power of God" (1 Cor 1:18).

Trying to explain this message without seeming like a complete fool is impossible. Later in the same passage, the Apostle Paul says,

> "For the foolishness of God is wiser than men, and the weakness of God is stronger than men . . . but God chose what is foolish in the world to shame the wise. God chose what is weak in the world to shame the strong; God chose what is low and despised in the world, even things that are not, to bring to nothing things that are, so that no human being might boast in the presence of God" (1 Cor 1:27–29).

The truth is, there is always a temptation to feel shame when you preach the gospel. It is normal. The gospel is crazy, but it is also powerful. So don't be ashamed of the gospel (Rom 1:16). Being ashamed is why you sometimes get weird.

NO CHRISTIAN JARGON ALLOWED!

This means that Christian jargon and church words need to be left out of the conversation. Keep theological and biblical words in the mix, but make sure they're defined. For example, here are some common Christian clichés:

"The Lord laid it on my heart."
"I'm just blessed."
"I've been saved."

"In the flow of the Spirit . . ."
"We are going to love on them."
"I feel called."
"Hedge of protection . . ."
"Traveling mercies . . ."

When conversing with non-believers, all of these phrases need to go. People don't know what you're talking about. If you evangelize people using these words and phrases, they will just think you are talking some kind of weird, insider, cultish language. Instead, use words average people use.

As an example, I've been in situations where I'm talking to a non-believer, and a Christian friend interrupts. Any time I evangelize someone, I try to be calculated with my words and attentive to what the person is saying; however, I've had Christian friends roll up and start using churchy phrases, such as "The Lord has laid it on my heart to come over here and tell you about what God has done in our church, and you should know it's really great to be saved." It makes me uncomfortable, and it makes the person I'm evangelizing uncomfortable, too. I can sense the awkward tension that begins to develop with the non-Christian. But the Christian walks away having no clue that they just dropped a Christian-ese bomb on an otherwise fruitful encounter.

In an evangelistic conversation, I would probably never say, "The Lord laid it on my heart," because non-believers don't have a context for what the heck that means. I would simply say, "Hey, man, I wanted to tell you something." Use words that will make sense to them. Another phrase Christians often use is, "We're going to love on them," or, "We just wanted to love on you." What do you mean by that? That phrase will probably make no sense to them and will probably freak them out. Instead of saying that, just say, "Hey, I was wondering about you, tell me a little bit about yourself." Use wording you know they'll understand.

IF YOU USE THEOLOGICAL TERMS, EXPLAIN YOURSELF

I am not saying that we should stop using theological and biblical words. These are helpful to explain the realities of the gospel. We just need to spend some time explaining them in a simple way. Let's say you're doing evangelism and you say something like this. "You're a law-breaking, covenant-breaking depraved sinner. You need to be justified by the unmerited grace of God. Before you do this, regeneration needs to take place; you will be granted repentance, and you will be drawn to Christ and his substitutionary salvific work. You will then begin the process of sanctification leading to ultimate glorification with the multitude of saints and angels before the throne. Do you want to bow before his majesty right now?" Yeah, that's not going to be helpful. I know that was an exaggeration, but I have heard super theological guys attempt evangelism with similar words, and it gets weird.

If you know your theology, that's great. Just make sure to explain terms in a simple way. For example, justification is defined as "an instantaneous legal act of God in which he (1) thinks of our sins as forgiven and Christ's righteousness as belonging to us and (2) declares us to be righteous in his sight."[13] However, I would never describe justification that way to an unbeliever. When I use theologically meaningful words, I just explain them as simply as I can.

Here's an example of how I've defined justification. My friend Josh has an extremely broken past and is having a hard time forgiving himself and believing God could forgive him. I told him that the Bible talks about this concept called, "justification"—that when we believe in Jesus Christ as our Savior, God says we are forgiven and righteous. Jesus absorbs all our sins and mistakes in his death on the cross, and all of his perfection and obedience is declared to be ours.

With justification defined, I told him there is nothing he could ever do to save himself. Jesus has done everything that is needed, and he can be justified in the sight of God. And when he's justified, even his own opinion of himself doesn't ultimately matter. God will forgive him through Christ, and when he fully realizes that, he will be able to forgive himself.

By the end of our conversation, Josh was in a flood of tears and told me it all sounded "too good to be true." I then asked him, "but you hope that it is true, right?" And he said, "Yes." So don't shy away from theological words in evangelism, they have power. Just explain the words well and don't get weird.

THE HOT TUB GUY

Let me give you one final illustration to drive this point home. My wife recently got me a hot tub for Christmas. Soaking in a hot tub is a great way to decompress after a stressful day, and I'm definitely thankful for it. But getting the hot tub running required some basic maintenance knowledge. So the guy from the hot tub store came to my house to talk to me about setting things up and getting the water chemicals straight. He had expertise, and I had interest. We were both motivated by all things hot tub.

We went out to the back of the house with all the chemicals, and he started in on this long, elaborate explanation about hot tub maintenance. He used big words. I even took notes! But there was one significant problem. There was a huge gap between his knowledge and mine. He was motivated to teach, and I was motivated to learn; however, he kept losing me with complicated, technical jargon.

Throughout the conversation, I'd stop him to ask clarifying questions. His attempt to be thorough only muddied the water further by piling on more technical words about the chemicals and mathematical equations. I was thoroughly confused. My eyes started glazing over, and I felt defeated.

At some point in the conversation, I just started nodding and smiling to get him out of my backyard as quickly as possible. I shook his hand, thanked him, and sent him on his way. Then I grabbed my computer, went on YouTube, and found a hot tub guy who explained things clearly. My point is this: sometimes your knowledge can be your worst enemy in evangelism. You need to remember that most of the time you are talking to people who have rarely, if ever, been inside of a church, have never cracked open a Bible, and have no idea what you mean by words like saved, gospel, redemption, Christian walk, sanctification, atonement, covenant, communion, baptism, or Deuteronomy.

ALWAYS BE PREPARED

Another thing that helps with the awkwardness of spiritual conversation is preparedness. In the same letter we discussed earlier, the Apostle Peter instructed the early Christians regarding their conversations with those outside the faith by saying, "but in your hearts honor Christ the Lord as holy, always being prepared to make a defense to anyone who asks you for a reason for the hope that is in you . . ." (1 Pet 3:15).

Do you see what Peter says there? In your hearts, regard Christ the Lord as holy. Always be prepared to make a defense—always. Be ready to talk about the hope that is in the gospel of Jesus Christ. You never know when the Holy Spirit is going to give you that moment. You need to be prepared. When you're not prepared, that's when you "get weird" with the dry mouth, the cold disposition, the big Bible words.

Start by honoring Christ inside yourself. This is what the Apostle Peter means when he says, "in your hearts honor Christ the Lord as holy." Peter refers here to internalizing the gospel. Let the reality of the holy Christ flood your heart. He is your Lord, your Messiah, your Savior, and your God. This is personal for you. So before you honor him in the presence of others by evangelizing, personally honor him in your heart. To do this, read passages about the gospel. Listen to how your pastor talks about the gospel, worship God, and pray that the Spirit gives you words to open their eyes.

The next thing Peter says is "be ready." You never know when you will have an opportunity to speak about Christ. If you are ready, you will have opportunities. You never know when the conversation will move from surface to depth, but when it does, be natural, and be yourself.

Next, and this is really important, step into the moments that you get with people. What I mean by this is when an opportunity comes to talk to someone about God, don't let the moment pass you by. Instead, step into it. I can think of opportunities I have had to speak about Christ that I passed up because I was not ready or I didn't step into the moment that I had. For example, when I was a new Christian I had a non-Christian friend tell me "I feel so far from God." I was not ready so I just said, "yeah, well you could come to church." I was not ready to help him connect to God. I got weird and awkward. Since then I have had dozens of conversations with him, and he will not even come close to the subject of God. So be ready to talk about your hope. Remember, you have good news! You have hope!

I could have asked him a few questions about what he meant and told him how the Bible answers those questions. I could have told about how many writers in the Bible felt the same way (Ps 13). I could have talked to him about the omnipresence of God. I could have talked to him about how Christ came near so that we would never be alone. I could have told him about the indwelling Spirit given to believers in Christ. I could have told him that God would hear him pray if he called out in his loneliness. I could have told him how he could come close to God through the person and work of Jesus as a perfect substitutionary priest. But I wasn't ready.

But there have been other conversations where I have been ready and able to talk to friends about the pain and emptiness that they feel and how God heals and fills those voids. I have shown atheist friends (who are now Christians) that they already live life based on intangible realities that are beyond the material universe. I have been able to tell criminals that God loves them and that Jesus became a criminal for them. All these things happened because I was ready to talk about my hope.[14]

What about you? You have hope in Jesus, or I doubt you would read this book. Are you ready to talk about it? It's not like you are talking about a burdensome religion. You are talking about hope. Hope in the Bible is a hope that is sure—something that is full of joy! That is why it is good that you are taking time to read this book. You can grow in being an ambassador of hope. Think of it as inviting a friend to come and discover some incredible breathtaking reality.

EVANGELISM IS INVITING PEOPLE TO A BEAUTIFUL HOPE

Lake Tahoe is 35 to 40 minutes from my house. Whenever someone visits Reno, I usually take them to Tahoe for lunch. The view never disappoints no matter how much I play it up. It is absolutely majestic. Its beauty always exceeds expectation. My friends are always in awe of the glory of the mountains, the blueness of the water, the scent of the pine, and the freshness of the air.

When we invite people to hope in Christ, it is the same. He always exceeds expectation—the infinite nature of his being, the freeness of his love, the costliness of his sacrifice, the depth of his forgiveness, and the comfort of his provision. He is hope. So we are free to talk about him in the highest of terms and the most elaborate language. We are free to be normal and not weird.

IT'S OK TO NOT ALWAYS HAVE THE ANSWERS

Another reason conversation with unbelievers gets weird is we get paranoid that we'll mess it up. You don't need to have everything figured out. If you don't have all the answers to people's questions, you can say something like, "I'm not sure, I'll have to look into that." Don't get weird, don't get defensive, and don't get frustrated.

If the gospel is true (and of course it is), then we should have no insecurities talking about it, just like we would talk about anything else that is true. You just say it in your way, with your personality, and in your opportunities.

Getting comfortable and confident in evangelism purely comes down to repetition. Like mastering a golf swing or parallel parking, the more you do it, the better you get. The more you talk about Jesus, the more comfortable you are going to be with these types of conversations. In the end, the one who has the power to draw people is God who is sovereign over your conversations and interactions with those who don't believe the gospel—it's not all up to you. Relax a little.

Remember that the Apostle Peter begins this instruction by saying, "in your hearts honor Christ the Lord as holy." In your hearts, always lift up Christ, always submit the conversation to him, and trust him! Ask the Holy Spirit to fill you up. When you speak, "do it with gentleness and respect, having a good conscience" (1 Pet 3:15–16).

After the conversation is over, trust Jesus for the effects of the conversation. Ultimately you are the messenger of the gospel, not the message itself. God is the one who ultimately evangelizes them and changes their hearts. So don't get weird.

CHAPTER 8

Invite People to Church

This morning, my son Tyler called me to ask what he should do to help teach one of his friends about God. In previous years, he'd spent a lot of time investing in his friend (we'll call him Adam). They were good friends and had many meaningful conversations. Soon after, Adam and his family moved nine hours south to Las Vegas.

Over the years, they've kept in touch through texting and social media. As I write this, just last night, Adam called Tyler amidst a crisis of faith. The first thing to learn from this is that sometimes when you plant a seed, it takes years before it pops out of the ground. The following is essentially what I told him.

INTRODUCING PEOPLE TO GOD'S WORD AND GOD'S PEOPLE

God has given us his Son and his word to know about him. First, God has given us his Son. Jesus said, "If you have seen me, you have seen the Father" (John 14:7). Jesus himself is also called the "Word of God" (John 1:1–14). Here's how all this relates:

When we speak with others, we use words. A word is a rational expression of an idea, reality, or fact. God spoke with us through the word that he gave to us in his Son, Jesus, who became human. I told my son to share with his friend everything he knows about Jesus, and in the process, his friend will learn about God.

God has also given us his word, the Bible. Read passages of Scripture with the person you're evangelizing and talk through the passages together.

In addition, maybe the easiest way to introduce friends to God is to introduce them to God's people. In other words, invite them to church. When we're at church, we experience God's presence as his people worship through the preaching of the word, through baptism and communion. Seeing how God reveals himself through broken and imperfect people seems to help put things into context and make ideas and concepts stick.

I happen to know a few pastors in Las Vegas, so my son and I worked together to figure out which church to invite his friend to. When you find a church where the gospel is preached, the church of Jesus Christ is the single most effective evangelistic strategy on planet earth. The church engages a person on every level—intellectually, emotionally, and relationally. Ideally, a church service gives someone an experience where there is time and safety to explore the claims of Christ.

Your calling as a Christian living in this world is to introduce people to God. You do this by inviting them to explore God, while you trust that God will work on their hearts when you do. Your job is not their conversion, but to introduce them to God and his people.

Just like I told my son above, you can extend three invitations to people so they're able to explore the realities of God. There's no particular order because one always leads to the other. These three invitations are to:

- Invite people to God's Son
- Invite people to God's word
- Invite people to God's church

INVITE PEOPLE TO GOD'S SON

Your main goal in evangelism is to get people to Jesus. You are not really trying to get them to accept your viewpoint, morals, political party, or your culture. You are trying to get them to understand who Jesus is. In your conversations with non-Christians, try to tell them everything you can about Jesus, including who he is, what he said, how he related to others, and how he healed people.

It's easy to get distracted with philosophical, ethical or religious arguments. But stay on point. Your job is to subtly, tactfully, but continually steer the conversation back to Jesus Christ. There are two ways to steer them to Christ: historically and personally. Both are essential to impacting any person you are evangelizing. When you point them to history, you are pointing people to objective truths. When you point them to your story, you point people to subjective truths. Here's what I mean.

Historically, steer them back to the Bible, explaining what Jesus did and said when he entered space and time. Without question, Jesus is the most significant man who has ever lived, and he has had the biggest impact on the world of anyone, ever.

Also, steer them to Christ personally. Tell them your story. Tell them how you have experienced Christ in the past, and how you experience him now. Tell them how he has provided for you. Tell them about the ways he has changed your perspective on life and has changed your desires.

The thing is, no one can really argue with your story. Often it's one of the most impactful parts of pointing people to the historical realities of the gospel. So, keep the objective history and your subjective story in mind, and this will help guide you in pointing others to Jesus Christ. Of course when you steer people to Jesus Christ, you will be steering them to his word and his church as well.

INVITE PEOPLE TO EXPLORE GOD'S WORD

Another effective strategy to invite people to explore God is to invite people to look into his word. There are three ways that have been useful for me in doing this. The first way is what I call, "you read; we talk." The second is, "we read; we talk." The third way is to invite them to a Bible Study, community group, or something similar.

If you can get someone interested in the "you read, we talk" phase, they are likely self-motivated in regards to study. For example, you might suggest that you both read Mark 1–3 and get together over coffee to talk about it. You can suggest they write down their thoughts and questions, and you will do the best you can to answer them.

The second way—"we read, we talk"—involves getting together to read a passage of Scripture together and ask questions of the text. Through your discussion together, you can lead them to the meaning of the text.

The last way is to invite them to some sort of Bible Study group. This could be a community group, missional group at your church, some sort of evangelistic Bible study, or new believer's class at your church. Then, make yourself available to further discuss the Scriptures with them. When you do this, it will inevitably lead to Jesus and discussion of the community of Jesus, his church.

INVITE PEOPLE TO GOD'S CHURCH (BUT REMEMBER THAT IT CAN FEEL INTIMIDATING)

Inviting your friend to church is probably the simplest form of evangelism. When they accept your invitation, I recommend you either meet them in the parking lot, ride to church together, or save an open seat next to you. Remember, showing up to a church can be extremely intimidating for people who aren't used to attending, or have never attended at all.

Think about it, if someone invited you to go to a Buddhist temple, how intimidated would you be? You would be questioning the whole situation. And consider the added anxiety if they have kids they'll be sending to children's church. Put yourself in their shoes. Imagine the nerves you'd have sending your kids to be in a Buddhist kid's classroom! You'd be asking yourself a number of questions. What do I wear? How do I act? What do I do when I get in there? Are they going to point me out? What kind of rituals am I going to experience? Is everyone going to know that I don't belong? Will these people like me? Are they ok with me disagreeing with some of this stuff? Do I need to give money? Put yourself in their shoes and do everything that you can to ease their fears. Don't let anything be a stumbling block. Jesus himself is an already big enough pill to swallow.

BRINGING FRIENDS TO CHURCH IS EFFECTIVE EVANGELISM

Statistics say bringing a friend to church might be the most effective evangelistic strategy. In one study, "more than 50,000 people over the last 10 years were asked why they came to church, and between 75% and 90% of respondents say, 'I began attending because someone invited me personally.'"[15] That number is astonishing! Between 75% and 90% of people who come to Christ became a Christian because someone invited them to church. We must remember that the church is specially designed by God to not only mature people in Christ, but to lead people to Christ. The Apostle Paul taught us that church services should be somewhat evangelistic and inviting to unbelievers. "But if . . . an unbeliever or outsider enters, he is convicted by all, he is called to account by all, the secrets of his heart are disclosed, and so, falling on his face, he will worship God and declare that God is really among you" (1 Cor 14:24–25).

I can't even begin to tell you how many people have become Christians and been baptized because someone in our church invited them. Often visitors come for a while, experience the community, experience public worship, hear gospel sermons, and eventually bow their knee to Christ.

While inviting others to church should not be our only evangelistic tool, it might be the most effective. This is one of the reasons why I have given a significant amount of my life to church planting. C. Peter Wagner asserts, "Planting new churches is the most effective evangelistic methodology known under heaven."[16] I believe it is the most effective evangelistic strategy there is. As Tim Keller has said,

> The vigorous, continual planting of new congregations is the single most crucial strategy for (1) the numerical growth of the body of Christ in any city, and (2) the continual corporate renewal and revival of the existing churches in a city. Nothing else—not crusades, outreach programs, para-church ministries, growing mega-churches, congregational consulting, nor church renewal processes—will have the consistent impact of dynamic, extensive church planting. This is an eyebrow raising statement, but to those who have done any study at all, it is not even controversial.[17]

So, in summary, invite them to church because the church is God's chosen mechanism in the world to draw in his people.

INVITE YOUR FRIENDS TO CHURCH AT CHRISTMAS AND EASTER

There are a couple of strategic times in the year when your friends and neighbors are more likely to attend church if you invite them. These are obviously Christmas and Easter. My wife has been great at this. For the past several Christmases and Easters, she has invited lots of folks from my kids' school—other moms and dads, teachers, and principals as well as surrounding neighbors.

There have even been times when a whole row or two of people attend one of these services because she invited them. After their first encounter with the church, some began attending on a somewhat regular basis, following the sermons online, or asking about church the next Christmas or Easter.

One person she invited even began attending church every week, giving financially, and is considering baptism. All this resulted because my wife, Rachael, simply invited people she's in relationship with. In other words, it all began with her being a friend of sinners.

Remember, when you invite someone to church, it might take awhile before they show up for the first time. And if they do come, it might take some regular attendance before they begin asking questions.

Being a friend of sinners means you are willing and ready to take the journey with them. And the journey is often three steps forward, two steps back, and repeat. This journey requires your love and patience, but know this: when you invite them to church, you are putting your confidence in God, the preaching of his word and the transforming power of the gospel. I've seen the baptismal waters filled and stirred hundreds and hundreds of times at our church. And it all started with someone who was willing to be a friend of sinners and invite someone to explore God with them. Being an evangelistic friend of sinners is being an inviter. So don't be afraid to invite your friends to Jesus, the word, and the church.

CHAPTER 9

You Are Not Jesus

#Evangelism is primarily about communication
of good news not execution of good works.
Good works without good news is not
#evangelism.

In this little book we've covered a lot of ground on what
evangelism is and how to do it. My hope is that you've
learned something along the way and that evangelizing is
really just a willingness to be a friend to sinners, like Jesus is.

What I am about to say in this chapter I will say multiple
times and in many different ways. It is repetitive, but this
is intentional because I believe it is imperative. This chapter
is about the misconceptions around a concept that has been
stuck to the Christian culture like a piece of gum on the

bottom of your shoe. It needs to be dug at and scraped off once and for all, and it'll take a little more time and effort. It has to do with the common teaching that our lives are the gospel. Yes, our actions can be persuasive, and we can be good citizens and loving neighbors, but we ourselves are never the gospel. Hang in there and allow me to explain.

THE GOSPEL IS NEWS ABOUT JESUS

"But when the goodness and loving kindness of God our Savior appeared, *he saved us, not because of works done by us in righteousness*, but according to his own mercy, by the washing of regeneration and renewal of the Holy Spirit, whom he poured out on us richly through Jesus Christ our Savior" (Titus 3:4–6, emphasis mine).

First and foremost, the gospel is news. News has to be announced, communicated, written, and delivered with words. Think of any major news story or event: the reporter doesn't seek to act it out. They aren't doing anything to make the news true; they're simply delivering a message. A reporter recounts an event that happened in space and time. Even if the news report is followed by a video, it's a video of the event possibly accompanied by words explaining the event. The gospel is news about an actual historical event accomplished by a historical person that has altered history. Jesus did something that changed everything. The New Testament was written in Greek, and the Greek word for our English word "gospel" means "good news." As one official definition puts it, the definition of this Greek word as it is set in the New Testament context is "good news concerning the now present instantiation of Jesus' divine dominion and way of salvation by his death and resurrection."[18]

THE GOSPEL IS NOT NEWS ABOUT YOU

Here's some more good news. The gospel is not news about you and what you have done to be good. It's news about Jesus. You are simply a beneficiary of this news and a recipient of this news, but you are not the news. This is good news because you and I could never be good enough to bring ourselves salvation, let alone bring salvation to anyone else by our own goodness. Evangelism is about announcing the goodness of another. It's about announcing the historical reality that the goodness of Jesus brings rescue to weary sinners. That is what makes it good news! It is an announcement about a historical reality. Jesus lived, died, and rose again for you and me.

This is why I find it so confusing when I hear people say things like, "we're just trying to live the gospel," or "we're trying to be the gospel." Another way of putting this is that Christians often believe it's their good works, their moral living, or their method of evangelism that is the gospel. I'm all for good works, holiness, Christian obedience, mercy ministries, and social justice. In fact, I lead a church that is "in the city, for the city," but we know that slogan represents good works only and should not be confused with good news.

Without a doubt this good news could have an effect that could change someone's world. But if you do evangelism by trying to "be" the gospel, not only will you be guilty of false advertising (you're not the Savior), but nobody will hear the real good news about Jesus Christ. Only Jesus could live out the gospel and be the gospel (don't burden yourself). At the very heart of the gospel is that none of us can "be" the gospel or "live" the gospel. This is why we need the one who can and did. That is, there is very "bad news." You have fallen short of the glory of God (Rom 3:23). We have lived out the "bad news" part, not the "good news" part.

Although this might rub you the wrong way at first, this is actually really good news if you are someone committed to evangelism! You don't have to be Jesus! You can (and will) struggle with sin, doubt, and personal weakness and still do evangelism because you don't have to be perfect to do it. Jesus was perfect on your behalf, and this is part of your proclamation. Being a good evangelist isn't about how moral you've been—it's about reporting on the historical realities of Jesus' life, death, resurrection, and all that means for sinners. It's this very news that changes the course of people's lives. You can tell them about how God has changed you in your desires, affections, and behaviors without trying to be the perfect gospel.

OBEDIENCE TO THE LAW IS NOT THE GOSPEL

Getting the focal point of the gospel straight is huge in rightly understanding evangelism. As I have talked to Christians over the years, they often fear that their life doesn't match the message and that this can be a significant barrier to doing evangelism. They're right, of course. None of us live as we ought to 100% of the time. If you think you are worthy to earn the gospel based on your moral performance, you have never studied the law of God. "For by the works of the law no human being will be justified in his sight" (Rom 3:20). Just take a moment to think about the Ten Commandments (Exod 20). The heart of the gospel message is that "now the righteousness of God has been manifested apart from the law . . . the righteousness of God through faith in Jesus Christ for all who believe" (Rom 3:21–22).

The gospel is something that is apart from the law of God. Your obedience to God's law is not the gospel. The gospel is the gospel. And the gospel is that Jesus obeyed the law on our behalf, died for our disobedience to it, and rose again to give us the Holy Spirit to pursue obedience in it. No one is worthy but Jesus Christ, and he fulfilled all that you need in your place. Now you're free to tell others about this grace. Even those Christians that seem to have it all together likely struggle with more "acceptable" sins like gossip, slander, bitterness, performance, judgmentalism, works righteousness, prayerlessness, or pride. Every one of us needs the grace that we preach. This reality actually spurs us on in evangelism; it doesn't discourage it.

GOOD DEEDS NEVER SAVED ANYONE

There is of course the well-known quote often attributed to St. Francis of Assisi, "Preach the gospel at all times, and if necessary, use words." This is clever, but not biblical. To put it in theological terms, this is a confusion of the distinction between law and gospel. It's a confusion between sharing the good news of what Jesus has objectively done for sinners (the gospel), and what God calls us to do in order to serve and love our neighbors (the Great Commandment, Matt 22:36–40). So the assumption of that quotation is that the gospel is something we live through our actions of love toward our neighbor. But our loving actions are not the gospel.

My argument is that it's always necessary to use words, because the gospel is news about Jesus, not works done by us. The gospel centers on who Jesus is and what Jesus did and does. The gospel is the good news that God sent his perfect Son, Jesus Christ, to live, die, and rise again on behalf of sinners, to save their souls and reconcile them to God. The gospel is expressed in his person (God and man), his works (obedience and submission to God on our behalf), his death (in our place and for our sins), and his resurrection (to grant us new life). That is the gospel. You see, who you are and the things you do did not make the cut to be included in the news of the gospel. You are not Jesus, and you don't need to try to be Jesus.

I love the quote attributed to Martin Luther that says, "God doesn't need your good works, but your neighbor does." That's a power-packed statement. Luther is saying in part that God is already satisfied with Jesus' work for you. So you don't have to do good in order to be in God's good graces. Once a Christian is accepted by God on account of Jesus, he gets to freely love his neighbor, not for his own benefit, or even God's, but for their neighbor's benefit!

Good works, obedience to God's word, and repenting of sin are all necessities, but care for the poor, love for our cities, and love for our neighbors never made anyone become a Christian. No one enters into eternal life because we gave somebody a sandwich or they saw our "holy" lives. People get saved because they hear the preaching of the good news of Jesus. Our good works can give us a credible platform to preach the gospel, but our good works are not the gospel. The gospel is the gospel. Jesus and his good works constitute that message. In other words, good works without good news do no eternal evangelistic good. In Titus 2:1, the Apostle Paul instructs Titus to "teach what accords with sound doctrine" and then describes Christian works and behavior. At the end of this section, he tells Titus that these good works "adorn" the doctrine of the gospel. Notice Paul's distinction between Christian works and the gospel: "showing all good faith ["all good faith" is the Christian behavior described in verses 2–9], so that in everything they may *adorn the doctrine of God our Savior*" (Titus 2:10, emphasis mine).

Then, he tells us what that doctrine is, he calls the gospel the "grace of God" that has appeared. Notice that it is historical news about Jesus that brings a righteous change to our lives.

> For *the grace of God has appeared, bringing salvation for all people,* training us to renounce ungodliness and worldly passions, and to live self-controlled, upright, and godly lives in the present age, waiting for *our blessed hope, the appearing of the glory of our great God and Savior Jesus Christ, who gave himself for us to redeem us from all lawlessness and to purify for himself a people for his own possession* who are zealous for good works (Titus 2:10–14, emphasis mine).

Paul told Titus that good works have their proper place when they adorn the gospel: "… but showing all good faith, so that in everything they may *adorn the doctrine of God our Savior*" (Titus 2:10, emphasis mine). Works follow and accompany gospel proclamation, but as I've been saying, works are not gospel proclamation. Never do Paul, Jesus, or any of the apostles tell us that our good works are the gospel. Good works that adorn good news do not only earthly good, but also eternal good. Jesus even said, "Let your light shine before others, so that they may see your good works and give glory to your Father in heaven" (Matt 5:16).

THE DIFFERENCE BETWEEN THE BODY OF EVANGELISM AND THE ADORNMENT OF EVANGELISM

Think of it this way: the gospel is the body of evangelism and good works are the clothing (adornment) of evangelism. Just as clothes are not as important as the person, human works are not as important to evangelism as the gospel. Clothing is extremely important and essential, but can quickly be replaced—a person cannot. Human works come and go with different quality, but the gospel happened 2,000 years ago perfectly! At the church where I lead, this is our strategy. We do good works as a platform for good news. We know, though, that our works are not the good news. We take care of the poor, engage in the arts, and help local schools. We do these things not as an end in themselves, but these things are all part of our strategy to proclaim the good news of the gospel to our city. They are a means to an end, but they are also good in themselves and a part of God's kingdom the world. These works are not the gospel.

I talk to so many people who go to the church where I pastor, and they tell me, "I'm just being really friendly and helpful. My friends know I'm a Christian. When they want to know about Jesus they'll ask me. My life speaks for itself." In response to that, I have to ask a few questions: "Did you believe because someone was nice? Did you conclude from their kindness that Jesus is God the Creator, you are a sinner in need of a Savior, and that Jesus died for your sin and rose from the dead as King? Did you conclude that God loves and forgives all who come to Jesus? Did you conclude that he will come again and bring a just kingdom to this world? Did you conclude that all who are not on the side of his grace will answer for their sin?" The answer of course is, "No." These people in your life will just think you are nice and continue to walk in darkness.

Do you see? You and I are not the gospel; Jesus Christ is the gospel. There are four books in our Bible that we call gospels that detail him as the hero. You and I are not Jesus;

Jesus is Jesus. Therefore you cannot live or show the gospel; you must proclaim it. The gospel is a message that must be preached, proclaimed, and told using words. And now we're invited to speak with others about that good news. And this, in a nutshell, is evangelism.

Frequently Asked Questions in Evangelism

In this chapter, I'm going to do what I can to point you in the right direction on some of the frequently asked questions you will encounter during evangelism. One thing to remember when answering these kinds of questions is that if you get stumped, it's not really a problem. You're free to tell people you'll get back to them after you've had time to think about it. After years and years of evangelizing others, I often tell the person, "I don't really know, it's a mystery. We don't really know everything about God and his plans, which makes him God and us creatures." I have found that people actually appreciate when you don't act like a know-it-all. It's also okay to be honest about your own struggles and doubts. Remember, you're not trying to win them to the strength of your faith; you're trying to win them to "the faith" (Jude 3).

1. Isn't the Bible full of errors? How can you base your faith on something that is so full of contradictions?

There have been some magnificent works written answering these questions in detail. But when people ask that question, I first tell them: "I'm not aware of any outright contradictions or errors in the Bible." I point out that many people have devoted their lives to find contradictions and have either come out empty handed or become Christians in the process. I then go on to show them that many of the so-called contradictions are not really contradictions at all, they are just figments of imagination coming from people who left logic at the door because they don't want to believe that the Bible is true. Of course you wouldn't say it this way, but you want to humbly help them see that your faith is logical, historical, and trustworthy.

For example, people point out that Jesus' virgin birth is only discussed in two of the four gospels. Some scholars point out that this is clearly a contradiction. But I don't think it's a contradiction. It's actually quite simple. Mark and John simply don't mention it. It would only be a contradiction if they said, "Hey guys, Joseph had sex with Mary and conceived baby Jesus. We don't know what the heck Matthew and Luke were talking about."

Another issue I've heard comes from the accounts surrounding Jesus' resurrection. In Luke's Gospel, we are told that the women went to the tomb on the first day of the week (24:1). And at the tomb they discovered that Jesus' body was not there (19:55–24:3). In John's gospel we are told, "on the first day of the week, Mary Magdalene came to the tomb early, while it was still dark, and saw the stone and been moved" (John 20:1).

Again, certain people point out that this is clearly a biblical contradiction, and again it is obviously not. Somehow, though, this keeps ending up in university courses. Luke mentions that there were several women there, while John simply decides to highlight the fact that Mary Magdalene was there. John didn't say "Mary Magdalene was by herself, and no one went to the tomb with her." If he did, then we would have a contradiction. I could go on with these examples, but I think you understand what I'm getting at. The errors and contradictions are not really errors or contradictions.

2. How can we trust the Bible about what it says about God and Salvation? Doesn't it also condone slavery, murder, polygamy, and genocide?

When people ask this question, the first thing I do is point out that the Bible tells us what happened historically and that many of the things that happened are not condoned by the Bible.

For example, the very center of the story of the Bible is the murder of the Son of God, and that murder leads to the redemption of all things. The biblical story explains how God used this atrocity for our good and his glory. But the Bible nowhere condones killing God's Son. In the same way, the Bible reports for us that there were murders, genocide, and slavery. But everything in the biblical story tells us by commands and consequences that these things are evil.

In regards to slavery, God even gave commands to regulate slavery to ensure that it did not get as evil as it could (although slavery in New Testament times was not like the slavery that we know of in North American history). It carried more of the idea of an indentured servant. But nowhere does God say that slavery was a good thing. In fact, it was a thorough, careful study of the Bible that led Christians to begin the abolitionist movement in the 1700s and 1800s.

Even the best of people in the Bible made huge mistakes, massive sins that had terrible consequences. Reporting what happened is not condoning what happened. There is only one hero in the Bible: Jesus Christ. Everyone else is in need of that hero. The Bible is not a story of good guys and bad guys. The

Bible is a story of a Good God who sent a Good Guy to give bad guys grace.

In summary, the Bible does not condone slavery, murder, polygamy or genocide. It reports that these things happened.

3. If I become a Christian, don't I have to give up science? What about fossils, the big bang, and evolution?

This is not a battle we Christians need to fight on. Here's one helpful thing to keep in mind and share with those you witness to: all of us presuppose things about the Bible before we even begin reading. We need to do the hard work of aiming to understand the intended meaning of the text. We might ask ourselves questions like: What did the author intend to communicate? Who was the original audience? What genre is this? Think of it this way—why would we go looking for love poetry in a nation's constitution? Likewise, we can't go looking for science in a text aiming to show God's covenant people that there is no other god but him.

You see, we can't cram our presupposed ideas into a text and hope to make sense of it. And this is often the case when it comes to questions of science in the Bible. Once we lay this groundwork, we need to remind people that the central issue is that Jesus lived, died, and rose again. I just tell people that nothing in the Bible contradicts anything in science. I also tell them that there are some well-meaning, crazed, fundamentalist interpretations of the Bible that don't allow for much science. But whatever we find in the world scientifically was put there by God, and there's nothing in the Bible that would contradict that. I also mention that depending on the way you interpret Genesis—as poetry or prose—you can come up with six literal days of creation or allow room for something like evolution. I tell them I don't believe in evolution—not because of anything in the Bible, but because I'm not convinced by the science of it. It seems to me that most of it is based upon theory and not true evidence, and science by its very nature is evidentiary. But I also tell them that I have friends that believe in every word of the Bible and believe in evolution, and then I tell them about Jesus.

4. What about dinosaurs?

For some reason I get asked this question a lot. I believe in dinosaurs. Nothing in scripture contradicts their existence, and I'm not sure why people keep asking.

5. Why are there so many different religions?

When people ask this question, I tell them that, at the end of the day, I don't know why there are "all of the religions." I explain that, from the beginning, ever since sin entered the world, false religions have developed. The major difference between false religions and the true faith in Jesus Christ is this: All religions are systems designed to get you to God, but the gospel of Jesus is the opposite. It is God coming to you. Other religions could be symbolized by ladders that ascend into heaven that you are required to climb. Our faith is symbolized by a cross coming down from heaven.

6. Why are there so many different denominations of Christianity? What is the difference between Baptist, Jehovah's Witness, Lutheran, Assemblies of God, Presbyterian, Mormon, Roman Catholic, and Episcopalian?

This question can be a little bit tricky, because out of the list above, two are cults. The various different denominations— Baptist, Lutheran, Assemblies of God, Presbyterian, Roman Catholic, Episcopalian, and many others—are all Christian denominations that hold to the same core doctrine of things like the Trinity, Virgin Birth, Jesus' death and resurrection, Jesus' return, and salvation through faith (except for Catholics); however, they differ on things we might refer to as second and third ring doctrine. These second or third ring doctrines are things like baptism, spiritual gifts, how to "do church," church leadership structures, and the role of women in the church. Denominations also differ on what would be considered preferential traditions, like what kind of building you meet in, what kind of clothes you need to wear to church, what kind of music you incorporate in your services. All of these denominations hold to the core of the Gospel that we have defined above in this book, along with the Apostle's Creed. These are all Christian groups that we as Christians would consider as our brothers and sisters in Christ. Some have very minor differences, and others have major differences. Consider these to be flavors of Christianity that flow from different people groups and reach different kinds of people in history and around the world through these differences. But at the core there is the same gospel outlined in the Apostles Creed.

The other two that I didn't list—Mormons and Jehovah's Witnesses, along with other cults—are not Christian. This is because they do not believe in the Christian Gospel and do not hold to the Apostle's Creed. They use the same words other Christian groups use, but have different meanings for each of those words. For example, when a Christian speaks of Jesus Christ, we mean the God-man (100% God and 100% man). When a Mormon speaks of Jesus Christ, they mean a god among many gods, who is the son of the father god of this world and the brother of Satan. When a Jehovah's Witness speaks of Jesus Christ, they mean Michael the Archangel and not God at all.

7. I'm a good person, isn't that all that God cares about?

On one hand, I know what is meant when people say this. Yes, you are a "good person." You are made in the image of God, and in that sense every human being has goodness in them. And there's even another level where that is true. You might be able to say you are good compared to "bad people." Depending on which measuring stick you use, if you want to use the measuring stick of outward actions and breaking civil laws, then it might be true that you are good or better than others. But if we were to use the measuring stick of what is in each of our hearts before the face of God, all of us fall short of true goodness.

If it were only a matter of comparing one another with one another you might have an argument; for example, if you were to compare yourself with Hitler, or the guy on the news who robbed the liquor store and then physically assaulted a teenage girl on the way out. You can make the argument that since you don't do that kind of thing, you are good.

But when the Bible talks about good, when God talks about good, the standard is much different. Goodness in the Bible is defined by the perfect character of God. So it's not a matter of goodness as we humans who are flawed would see it, but it's a matter of goodness as a perfect God would see it. And in that sense the Bible says no one is good. For example, consider Paul's explanation in Romans 3:

- "None is righteous, no, not one" (here, he indicts the entire human race)
- "No one understands" (our minds are flawed).
- "No one seeks for God" (our wills are flawed).
- "All have turned aside; they have become worthless" (our value is flawed).
- "No one does good, not even one" (our morals are flawed).

- "Their throat is an open grave; they use their tongues to deceive . . . Their mouth is full of curses and bitterness" (our speech is flawed).
- "Their feet are swift to shed blood; and their paths are ruin and misery and in the way of peace they have not known" (humans have destroyed well-being).
- "There is no fear of God before their eyes" (we have forgotten God).

I'll also explain further to a non-Christian friend, "Now I know you do not accept the Bible as authority, but if you watch the news and see the human race and observe your own life that's pretty much what you're going to find, that humans are a mixture of beauty and brokenness. And on this point, I think the Bible is pretty accurate, and even if you look at your own heart, you have to admit that there are things about yourself that you're ashamed of, that you wish you could change, things you are guilty of, and you feel trapped by them. What the Bible tells me is that you need someone to save you because you can't ever be good enough to save yourself."

When we presuppose that our moral goodness factors into our relationship with God, by default, we're believing that we're in some sort of negotiation with God. Like there's some sort of transaction, as if God grades on a curve and rewards us for our good behavior. But a key truth of the Christian faith is that everything comes to us as pure gift. You see, we can't earn righteousness with God. We receive it from him on account of Jesus.

8. Don't all paths lead to God? Can't I just make my own way and decide what is best for me?

The first thing I point out to someone who says this is that none of the major world religions believe this. All of the major world religions teach exclusivity. They claim their path is the path to salvation.

The other thing I point out, is that if you're going to agree that all paths lead to God, and that whatever you decide to be true will be true, you have to accept that even those who adhere to radical Islam are correct in their pursuit of God. They believe that all infidels need to be killed and wiped off the face of the earth. The results of this belief are the terrible events in Brussels, Paris, Turkey, and the many places where Islamists have bombed people in the name of God; however, I doubt most people would agree that this path leads to God.

Who gets to be the judge over these paths? You? Or me? Or could it be that there is a higher being that makes these decisions? Deep down we know that there is something greater than us because we both agree that radical Islam is not a path. Isn't excluding any path, even if it's what you consider to be a harmful path, excluding something? By doing that, you are doing the same thing you claim religion should not do. By making this exclusion, you make the gate to heaven narrower than everyone. Isn't it worth listening to what Jesus has to say on the subject? I'm not saying that my opinion is better than your opinion, but I am saying that we could both benefit from listening to Jesus' opinion.

9. Christians are just as bad as anyone else (common examples are the Crusades, church scandals, or religious oppression), what gives you the right to tell me what the truth is?

First of all, I would agree that Christians are as bad as everyone else—everyone needs the Savior. But when someone argues that Christians don't have credibility due to bad morals, they are presupposing that Christianity is about morals. But it's not. It's primarily about the objective, historical truth of Jesus' death and resurrection. It's a truth claim, not a sales pitch to live up to a moral code. Some may point to crusades and church scandals and religious oppression to disprove Christianity. I point to those things to prove Christianity. They prove Christianity because they show that all of us are in need of salvation and that even those who are pursuing the path of righteousness often end up in the middle of darkness doing dark things. The people who did those things didn't do them because they were living in obedience to Jesus and his gospel. But they did those things because they were out of alignment with Jesus and his gospel. I would never point at Christians to prove Christianity. If I did, no one on Earth would ever believe in the gospel. I point at Christ to prove Christianity. You're right, Christians have been guilty of all sorts of terrible things, but Christ was never guilty of one thing. He never sinned in thought, word, or deed. He never started a war, led a crusade of oppression, or enacted a scandal. Instead, he took upon himself all of our scandals and wars and sins against God.

10. If I follow Jesus Christ does that mean I have to go to church?

The short answer to that question is, "Yes." The only kind of Christianity is a church-based Christianity. Jesus saved a people, not just a person. Jesus has a body, not a body part. In all of Jesus' teaching, you cannot find any endorsement of "Lone Ranger" Christianity, and if you read the writings of the apostles, you will only find writings sent to Christians who were part of churches. To say, "I'm a Christian, but I don't go to church," is actually a theological impossibility. To be a Christian is to be a part of the Church. It is possible to be a disobedient Christian who disobeys Jesus and doesn't go to church. But in my experience, eventually Jesus will make sure you see things his way. Saying, "I love Jesus but I don't like the church," is like you saying to me, "Harvey, I love you but I don't like your wife. Can we be friends?" My answer to you would be emphatically, "No!" To receive me is to receive my wife. The Church is Jesus' bride. Jesus loves his Church to the point of dying for his Church. The Church and Jesus are a package deal. To embrace the perfect Jesus, you also have to embrace his broken bride.

11. How do I know that God exists?

Usually people object to the existence of God because they have never seen him, heard him, or tangibly felt him. In other words, he is intangible. He is not able to be experienced by the five senses, and so people say, "I can't believe anything I can't experience with my five senses."

You actually believe in all kinds of things that are intangible. In fact, you live your life based on things that are intangible. Your life is built on intangibles. Let me explain what I mean. When you were a kid, why did you play? You played because the way you enjoyed it and the way it made you feel. What is enjoyment? What is feeling? It's an intangible impression that from the earliest age you've built your life upon. If you look at our world, what is everybody after? Money, sex, or power. Why? Not because of the things themselves, but because of the intangible realities behind those things.

Why do you want money? You want money because it gives you comfort, security, and it provides options. But what is comfort? It's an intangible reality. What is security? It's beyond anything we can feel with five senses. Even the material goods you buy, why do you want those? You want them because of the intangible realities they point to, the way they make you feel, the thrill of buying them, or the experience in using them. The pleasure in having it, tasting it, sitting on it, driving it, or watching it drives your behavior. It's not really about the hardware that you can experience with the five senses. It's about the reality behind all of it.

What about sex? Certainly that's physical. But what is sex really about? Have you ever noticed that you have certain longings for it when you're lonely or stressed or excited? Sure, there's the physical side of it, but everybody that has had sex knows there's more to it than that—it involves significant emotion. Even people who try to pretend it's purely physical end up jealous and broken-hearted because of past lovers and sexual experiences. Sex is really all about the intangibles.

And what is power, but an experience of control? And what is control, but an intangible, emotional, mental, subjective reality? Sure it's connected to objective realities as well, but no one wants power for the objective reasons. Everyone wants power because of the subjective reasons.

All this to say, we already live our entire lives based on things that we cannot see or touch or taste or feel. Yet every decision we make and emotion we have is connected to those intangible realities. It's really not that hard to believe in an intangible God. In fact, you and I both know you already prayed to him and experienced him. Maybe it was a sunset or the smile of a child or the waves of an ocean or laughter over a good cup of coffee, but in that moment you knew that there was something good and perfect that is beyond this present moment. I would say you already believe that God exists; you just don't know it yet.

12. What about all those weird Old Testament laws? How can you trust what the Bible says about sexuality or the exclusivity of Jesus when it also commands you in the Old Testament not to wear clothing of mixed material, or to cut your hair in certain ways?

The first thing I would say is that I would compliment the person for being aware of passages like that in the Bible. This type of question might come up with 5% of those people I do evangelism with. But this type of question does come up enough that I wanted to put it in the book. Here is a typical response: the Bible says all kinds of things, but you have to understand what book you're reading in the Bible, what kind of literature it is, and who it is written to. Not everything in the Bible is written *to* us, although I do believe everything in the Bible is written *for* us. Some of those Old Testament laws which some might consider obscure, were very real for your average Jew living before the time of Christ. They were part of the Mosaic law, part of God's covenant with his people. But to say that those laws apply now in the same way they applied then would be to miss one of the obvious things about your Bible.

The Bible is divided into two sections: an Old Testament and a New Testament. The Old Testament tells us everything, pointing to and leading up to the first coming of Christ. The New Testament tells us about the coming of Christ and how he is coming again. After Christ has come, many of those old covenant ritual and ceremonial and civil laws are no longer in effect because they were calling God's people to live holy and set apart from the corrupt cultures around them. They were distinctive laws so God's people would know they were set apart, but also so the people of the surrounding cultures would know it. In the New Testament, Jesus comes and lives the holy life they were called to and then credits that holy life to us. Because of this exchange, we no longer have to have these set rules to make us distinctively set apart or holy. We are given Christ's holiness. While the moral parts of the law reflected in the 10 Commandments still apply, the ceremonial, civil, and ritual parts of the law were fulfilled in Christ. These old covenant laws are also no longer in effect because God's covenant is not just with the Jewish people, but with people called out from every nation. The things that are said about sexual ethics and the exclusivity of Christ are things that were said in both the Old and New Testaments and apply to all peoples in all times and in all contexts. Context is the key to understanding the Bible.

Tough Questions in Evangelism

1. What about homosexuality? Does God hate homosexuals? Do I have to stop being a homosexual to become a Christian?

Before I get into this question. I want to say a few words because this issue is such a cultural hot button. You definitely want to handle this question with sensitivity and grace. The first thing to affirm is that God loves sinners. That's what the gospel is all about. Whether they are homosexual sinners or heterosexual sinners is not really the issue at all. In fact, one thing I always say is that it seems odd to me to define yourself by your sexual orientation. As someone who was made in the image of God, I don't walk around saying, "Hey, I'm a heterosexual." I'm not who I sleep with, I am who God says I am.

So what about homosexuals? They are people made in the image of God who are loved by God, and just like every other person on earth, they are people in need of grace. Does God hate homosexuals? God hates sin; this is why Jesus died. God loves sinners; this is why Jesus died—end of story. If you do decide to follow Jesus, there are many things you will need to change. The first thing you'll need to change is to stop defining yourself by your sexual orientation. Not only is homosexual activity ethically out of bounds, but it is in direct contradiction to the way that God created humanity as masculine and feminine. Humanity is revealed as sexual beings different from each other, but also dependent on each other for human flourishing. Homosexuality is not something that builds up community and is not something that can physically build a society because there is no possibility of procreation in it. Therefore there is no human flourishing.

So, not only is homosexuality an ethical issue, but it is a constitutional issue in regard to the constitution of humanity. By being someone created in the image of God and placed within Christ, you are given a new identity as a child of God who was washed clean and forgiven. If you become a Christian, you'll also have to stop lying and repent when you do lie. No more gossip, you'll need to be loyal to your friends, commit to the mission of God, and humble yourself under his word. And will this affect your sex life? Oh yes. It will affect your sex life whether you are a heterosexual or a homosexual. When Jesus becomes your Savior, he also becomes your Lord. He is a package deal. And as Lord, he wants to be King over every area of your life. Having said that, I'm sure you'll still struggle with same-sex attraction. Almost every heterosexual Christian I know struggles with lust, so don't think you're going to be different.

I would also note that I do recognize that your struggle as a same-sex attracted person is unique in that these desires you have will never be fulfilled if you are choosing to live with Jesus as your Lord. I will also tell you that while this is a painful struggle for you to live with, you may find that other things you are called to give up become just as difficult or more difficult, such as pride or selfishness. Will you have to stop having sex with people you're not married to? Yes, just like me and all the other Christians that decided to follow Jesus. Jesus only has one place for sex and, by the way, it's the best place. It's in the context of covenant marriage between a man and a woman. I know that seems quite narrow, but he is God, and he did create the world, including your sexual organs. What about homosexual marriage? Jesus doesn't even recognize it as a marriage. The only thing he calls a marriage is between one man and one woman for one lifetime. I know it might seem like he's being rigid and narrow minded, but I promise you, he knows what's best. If you don't believe me and you're struggling to trust that, just remember him bleeding on the cross for you—for heterosexual sins, homosexual sins, lies, thefts, gossips, slanderers, religious sinners, and the self-righteous. He bled for us all. I understand you have to give up who you would like to have sex with for him, but he gave up his life for you. I'd say that's fair.

2. If God is all-powerful and loving, why do bad things happen?

Well, God is all-powerful and loving, and bad things do happen. The assumption to that question is that both can't be simultaneously true, and that's a logical fallacy. The reason this world is so broken and in so much pain is because of human sin. It all started with the fall of humanity in Genesis 3 when Adam and Eve sinned against God. It continues every day when humans rebel against God, his created order, and when we harm one another.

Every time a human sins, it compounds the effect of sin in the world. Now there are nearly 6 and ½ billion people on earth, and all of those people are sinning every day in thought, word, and deed. This means the world is going to be a mess. The reason why we even have any other kind of expectation of goodness is because God created this world with beauty in billions of ways.

When the question is asked, "why didn't the all-powerful God stop us? If he's loving, why does he allow for human sin to cause pain day in and day out?" On one hand, I can't pretend that I know the mind of God or the exact answer to that question. On the other hand, there seems to be some evidence that if God were to destroy sin and remove it from our experience, he would also have to destroy us. This is why he took Adam and Eve out of the Garden of Eden and didn't allow them to eat of the Tree of Life. If he had, that would mean humans would live forever away from him. Fortunately, God made a promise of how he was going to fix our problem. A perfect human was going to be destroyed for all human evil. This is what Christmas and Good Friday and Easter are all about. Christmas is about God coming into this broken world to redeem it, to heal it, and to save it. Good Friday is about God taking upon himself all of that suffering, every sin, cancer, hurricane, famine, rape, burglary, beating, and act of neglect. God is not indifferent to our pain. He took it on himself; he absorbed it in his person on the cross. At one moment, in a naked human body on a wooden cross in the Middle East, he was all-powerful and all-loving at the same time, solving all the problems that the world would ever know. Easter is the promise that he is making this world new and that everything that is sad will one day come untrue.

3. What about hell?

Hell is final justice for all evil. I don't think anybody wants to live in a world where there is no final justice for the evils that have happened throughout history. Hell is the place where God finally brings all of those things to justice. Deep in the human soul we all long for justice. We all want somebody to pay for the wrongs done to us and the wrongs that have been done to other people. We can't stand the thought of people getting away with it. We can't stand the thought of evil going unpunished. The reason we feel this way is because we are created in the image of God and God can't stand it either. Although the thought of hell sounds horrible, the thought of a universe without a hell sounds worse. Hell is a place God created for the devil and his rebellious angels (Matt 25:41). Humans who join the devil in his rebellion against God and refuse the mercy offered by God through Jesus Christ could join the devil and his angels in hell. There is no mercy for demons. But for the human race, God has provided a Savior, and on the cross he went to hell in our place (1 John 2:2; Rom 3:24–25). Whoever will trust him and attach themselves to him through belief in him will escape hell. This is what the Bible calls propitiation. Propitiation basically means that Jesus becomes our wrath-bearer or hell-taker. Some people are stunned by the wrath of God against sin and sinners in hell. But what is even more stunning is Jesus' death on the cross that proved God's love for sinners.

Final Word

I know I said at the beginning of the book that I intended to demystify evangelism, but now I want to say that, since we have covered the principles, there is much left to evangelism that is mystical. There is much about evangelism that will cause you to depend on the Holy Spirit and listen to his voice. Let's take a moment and, if you're willing and able in the place where you are reading this, get on your knees and ask God to make you a friend of sinners. Pray for specific people. Ask God to save them. Believe. Join Jesus in befriending sinners.

SUMMARIZING THE BOOK

1. Prepare yourself
Pray for: courage, the person, yourself.

2. Be yourself
God made you uniquely and saved you so that you can be you when doing evangelism. It will take you being you for you to reach those whom he wants you to reach.

3. Forget yourself
Don't let your self-talk, fear of rejection, and insecurities get in the way of the gospel. Be more concerned about them and being their friend than you are concerned about how you look or sound. Be present with them.

Endnotes

1. Charles Haddon Spurgeon, "A Sermon and a Reminiscence," *The Sword & The Trowel*, March 1873. *http://www.spurgeon. org/s_and_t/srmn1873.htm.*

2. This idea came from conversation with Matt Hudgins, a church planting resident at our church.

3. A better, more updated, translation is, "Abstain from every form of evil" (ESV). The idea is to avoid sin, not sinners.

4. For a more robust understanding of this concept, see Tim Chester, *A Meal with Jesus: Discovering Grace, Community, and Mission around the Table* (Wheaton, IL: Crossway, 2011).

5. Martin Luther, *St. Paul's Epistle to the Galatians* (Philadelphia: Smith, English & Co., 1860), 206.

6. J. I. Packer, "Introduction," in *The Death of Death in the Death of Christ*, by John Owen (London: Banner of Truth, 1959), 4–5, *http://johnowen.org/media/packer_quest_for_godliness_ch_8.pdf.*

7. Tim Keller, *Paul's Letter to the Galatians: Living in Line with the Truth of the Gospel* (New York: Redeemer Presbyterian Church, 2003), 2.

8. To help you know the gospel even more, listen to good gospel preaching, get in a Bible study or community group, and read and listen to the New Testament.

9. To pursue this further, see J. I. Packer, *Evangelism and the Sovereignty of God* (Downers Grove, IL: IVP, 2012).

10. For an excellent understanding of this parable, see Tim Keller, *The Prodigal God* (London: Penguin, 2012).

11. This probably means "all kinds of people" based on the context, which reinforces that God is passionate to gather his lost people. We are called to this as well.

12. Paul F. M. Zahl, *Grace in Practice: A Theology of Everyday Life* (Grand Rapids, MI: Eerdmans, 2007), 36.

13. Wayne A. Grudem, *Systematic Theology: An Introduction to Biblical Doctrine* (Grand Rapids: Zondervan, 1994), 723.

14. For an excellent must-read for any evangelist, see Tim Keller, *The Reason for God: Belief in an Age of Skepticism* (London: Penguin, 2008).

15. Rachel Willoughby, "3 Questions for Charles Arn," *Christianity Today*, March 2009, *http://www.christianitytoday.com/le/2009/march-online-only/3-questions-for-charles-arn.html*.

16. C. Peter Wagner, *Church Planting for a Greater Harvest* (Ventura, CA: Regal Books, 1990), 11.

17. Tim Keller, "Why Plant Churches?" (New York: Redeemer City to City, 2009), 1, *http://download.redeemer.com/pdf/learn/resources/Why_Plant_Churches-Keller.pdf*.

18. Thomas Sheldon Green, *Greek-English Lexicon to the New Testament* (Grand Rapids, MI: Zondervan, 1976).